Pieces of a Puzzle

Pieces of a Puzzle

Perspectives on Child Sexual Abuse

edited by Diane Hiebert-Murphy and Linda Burnside

Second in the Hurting and Healing Series on Intimate Violence
Co-published by Fernwood Publishing
and RESOLVE (Research and Education for Solutions to Violence and Abuse)

Editing: Eileen Young
Cover art: Deanna Hiebert
Design and production: Beverley Rach
Printed and bound in Canada by: Hignell Printing Limited

A publication of:
Fernwood Publishing
Box 9409, Station A
Halifax, Nova Scotia
B3K 5S3
and
RESOLVE
(Research and Education for Solutions to Violence and Abuse)
108 Isbister Building, University of Manitoba,
Winnipeg, Manitoba, R3T 2N2

Fernwood Publishing Company Limited gratefully acknowledges the financial support of the Department of Canadian Heritage and the Canada Council for the Arts for our publishing program.

Le Conseil des Arts du Canada | The Canada Council for the Arts

Canadian Cataloguing in Publication Data

Main entry under title:
Pieces of a puzzle: perspectives on child sexual abuse

Includes bibliographical references.
ISBN 1-55266-043-5

1. Child sexual abuse—Prevention.   2. Sexually abused children—Rehabilitation.   3. Incest.   I. Hiebert-Murphy, E. Diane (Elizabeth Diane)
II. Burnside, Linda

HV6570.4C3P53 2001   362.76   C00-901775-5

Contents

Foreword

Elly Danica

Child abuse, in all its forms, including sexual abuse, is an integral part of the very structure of society. It is not an isolated event in the lives of a few unlucky children. Statistics and the experiences of front-line workers attest to the prevalence of child abuse and neglect in all our communities. It is not an anomaly, much as we might wish it was.

All forms of child abuse trauma disenfranchise the victim in profound and multiple ways. Depression, addictions and failure to protect the next generation from abuse are often the legacy of childhood abuse. A disenfranchised person, who must spend her or his entire life coping with the residuals of childhood trauma, is not an equal citizen. Those of us who have been abused in childhood must maintain a disproportionate focus on our own immediate lives and issues simply to survive. Because the effects of the trauma absorb so much of our time and energy, too often we cannot give our children the nurturing we'd wish to provide for them, and maintain marriages or jobs. We are too often politically, economically and socially disenfranchised as a result. This disenfranchisement functions to support a society with an unequal distribution of both power and money. Such a social construction requires an underclass. Childhood abuse produces a disenfranchised underclass in every generation.

The results of abuse and neglect of children can't help but impact on the whole of the community. What sort of communities do we expect to build if we don't do everything possible to keep children and all vulnerable people safe? We have a strong rhetoric in our country about the need to care for and protect children. Yet we also have one of the highest child poverty rates in the "first" world. Why? It is infuriating to hear about cuts to programs that primarily serve women and children. Is tax relief for the wealthy really more important than adequate welfare payments to single mothers? Do banks and corporations need tax breaks more than mothers and children need adequate housing?

Most front-line workers can tell us that victims of childhood abuse trauma require long-term help just to cope with their lives. Offenders need lifelong programs to ensure that they do not re-offend. Yet we don't see enough federal and provincial funding committed to this goal. Providing funds for facilities is given higher priority than funding treatment and preventive programs. Why don't the politicians get it? How can we, as a society, be so short-sighted that we don't adequately fund treatment programs and early intervention?

It is greatly encouraging to read the present volume of essays, that furthers the task of examining the many aspects of childhood sexual abuse. What works in treatment and support for children, non-offending parents and siblings? How do perpetrators rationalize and conduct their offences against children? How can the effects of abuse on the children, the family and the community be managed? How can the courts better address the legal issues of child abuse? All of these questions and the issues they raise require ongoing study.

The goal must be to prevent abuse in all its forms. Society will need to change if more children and adults are to live healthy and joyful lives. This is an enormous project but we can see ways to begin it. First, we can demand that adequate public funding be allocated to research on, and programs for, the treatment and support of victims and offenders. We need the best minds and the most committed among us to address the issue of child abuse if we are ever to impact on the lives of children at risk of abuse, and offer prevention and protection to all children. The volume you are about to read describes some intriguing research and programs. More needs to be done. This is a fine contribution to the work.

Acknowledgments

This book is the result of the commitment of RESOLVE (Research and Education for Solutions to Violence and Abuse) to disseminate current research regarding violence and abuse. We acknowledge the support of RESOLVE for this project and express particular thanks to Jane Ursel, director of RESOLVE and Caroline Piotrowski, chair of the publication committee.

The collection of research and programs outlined in this volume are the result of numerous partnerships between community agencies and researchers working together to better understand child sexual abuse and respond to the problem in an effective manner. Most importantly, the research was only possible because of the willingness of individuals affected by sexual abuse to participate in the various projects and allow their experiences to be used to help us all learn more about the issue. We are grateful for the participation of these individuals as well as the agencies that were supportive of, and partners in, the research.

There are many individuals who assisted us in bringing this book to publication. A large number of reviewers graciously contributed their time and expertise by providing useful feedback to the authors on early drafts of the chapters. These reviewers included both community members (Jacqueline Bedard, Elizabeth Beaupré, Linda Fadden, Bill Harriott, George MacDonald and Linda Perry) and academics (Karen Busby, Pete Hudson, Rick Linden, Eveline Milliken, Marsha Runtz and Barry Trute). We wish to thank each one of them for their insightful and thoughtful comments. We also wish to thank Elizabeth Newton who provided useful feedback on the entire manuscript. We are especially grateful to Wayne Antony of Fernwood Publishing for his guidance throughout this project. Also, thanks to Eileen Young for editing the final manuscript, to Beverley Rach for design and production and to Debbie Mathers for typing the final changes to the manuscript. Special thanks to Shawna Adolfson, Nicole Gornik, Chelsey Hiebert, Maggie Hiebert and Sam Murphy for creative inspiration for our cover, and to Deanna Hiebert whose artwork we have used.

About the Contributors

Linda Burnside, M.Ed., is currently an assistant program manager with Winnipeg Child and Family Services. She has experience in child protection and sexual abuse treatment and has worked extensively as a sessional instructor at the University of Manitoba.

Rayleen V. De Luca, Ph.D,. is a professor in the Department of Psychology at the University of Manitoba, where she has been the Director of Clinical Training since 1993. Her clinical and research interests include child psychopathology, child abuse and victimization and treatment of victims and offenders.

Kelly Gorkoff, M.A., is a research associate at RESOLVE, a tri-provincial network on research and education for solutions to violence and abuse and lecturer in the Department of Sociology, University of Manitoba. Her research focus is on social programming and policy, with a specific interest in justice and violence issues.

Alana D. Grayston, M.A., is a lecturer in the Department of Clinical Health Psychology at the University of Manitoba and provides assessment and treatment services to children through the Child Development Clinic at Children's Hospital. She is presently completing her doctoral dissertation in the area of sexual abuse.

Diane Hiebert-Murphy, Ph.D., is an assistant professor in the Faculty of Social Work and Associate Director of the Psychological Service Centre at the University of Manitoba. Her research focus is family violence (including partner violence and child sexual abuse) and family centred practice with families with children with disabilities.

Christine Kreklewetz, M.A., is an interdisciplinary doctoral candidate at the University of Manitoba. She is currently completing her dissertation on incest survivor mothers and the intergenerational transmission of incest.

Lisa Sutherland, M.S.W., has been involved in the field of family violence and abuse prevention since 1987. Lisa currently lives in Red Deer, Alberta, where she plans to continue her social work practice and education.

Jane Ursel, Ph.D., is an associate professor in the Department of Sociology at the University of Manitoba and Director of RESOLVE, a tri-provincial network on research and education for solutions to violence and abuse. She is the director of a longitudinal study of the Winnipeg Family Violence Court and is involved in social policy analysis and development.

D. Kim Wilson, B.S.W., has worked for the Department of Social Services in Saskatchewan since 1976, and is currently the Program Manager for Child Protection and Treatment for the Regina Regional office. His professional interests include art and play therapy, as well as documenting the stories of young survivors of sexual abuse.

Introduction

Diane Hiebert-Murphy and Linda Burnside

Interest in child sexual abuse has existed since at least the 1890s when Freud noted a connection between such experiences and the psychological difficulties of his patients. Subsequently, however, the occurrence of child sexual abuse was denied and attributed to sexual fantasy (Masson 1984; Rush 1980). More recently, the feminist movement and the movement against child abuse have encouraged awareness of the sexual abuse of children (Finkelhor 1979). Increasingly, child sexual abuse has become a concern for practitioners and researchers.

Child sexual abuse refers to a sexual act imposed upon a child by an individual who is in a position of power or authority over the child. From a legal perspective, there are many different behaviours that are considered sexual abuse. In Canadian criminal law, sexual offences against children include, for example, sexual assault, sexual interference, invitation to sexual touching, sexual exploitation and exposure (Standing Committee on Justice and the Solicitor General 1993). Fundamental to this form of violence is the power differential between the perpetrator of the violence and the victim. This power may exist because the offender is older, uses coercion or force and/or is in a position of trust relative to the victim. In cases of intrafamilial sexual abuse, the offender is someone who is known to and trusted by the child and who often lives in the child's home—factors that contribute to the occurrence of sexual abuse due to the proximity, power and close emotional relationship of the offender to the child.

Research on the prevalence of child sexual abuse documents that it is a frequently occurring psychosocial problem warranting attention. These studies suggest that between 11 percent and 45 percent of women (Baker & Duncan 1985; Finkelhor 1979, 1984; Fromuth 1986; Kercher & McShane 1984; Russell 1983; Wyatt 1985) and between 3 percent and 9 percent of men (Baker & Duncan 1985; Finkelhor 1979, 1984; Kercher & McShane 1984) experience child sexual abuse. Canadian research suggests that between 18 percent and 24 percent of women (Bagley 1988; Bagley & Ramsay 1986; Bagley & Young 1988) and 8 percent of men (Bagley 1988) experience unwanted sexual acts in childhood. These figures certainly understate the prevalence of sexual abuse. While reporting laws have been implemented in many communities since the 1970s, many children do not disclose their abuse, and many disclosures are not reported to authorities (Everstine & Everstine 1989).

Since the "discovery" of child sexual abuse, much work has been done to explore the effects that this abuse has on the victims. Children who are sexually abused tend to display more behavioural and psychological difficulties than do children who are not abused (see Beitchman et al. 1991; Browne & Finkelhor 1986; Kendall-Tackett, Williams & Finkelhor 1993). For example, children who experience sexual abuse are more likely to show sexualized behaviour (e.g., Einbender & Friedrich 1989; Friedrich, Beilke & Urquiza 1987; White, Halpin, Strom & Santilli 1988), internalizing behaviour problems such as depression and anxiety (e.g., Conte & Schuerman 1987, 1988; Einbender & Friedrich 1989; Friedrich et al. 1987; Tong, Oates & McDowell 1987) and externalizing behaviour problems such as aggression and antisocial behaviour (Conte & Schuerman 1987, 1988; Einbender & Friedrich 1989; Friedrich et al. 1987; Tong et al. 1987). Research also documents the long-term effects of child sexual abuse (see Beitchman et al. 1992). Unfortunately, children who have been hurt and traumatized by sexual abuse often become distressed and struggling adults (Briere 1992), experiencing flashbacks, dissociation, emotional numbness, somatic problems such as headaches and abdominal pain, self-abusive behaviours and suicidal thoughts or attempts (Cameron 2000). There is convincing evidence that sexual abuse in childhood results in psychological and interpersonal difficulties that can extend well into adulthood.

Our increased awareness of the deleterious effects of child sexual abuse highlights the need for a social response to the problem. Action is required. Yet solving the problem of child sexual abuse is complex. To effectively respond to the issue we must first come to some understanding of why sexual abuse exists. As in other areas of family violence, there are multiple and competing explanations of the causes of child sexual abuse. One approach, the feminist model, focuses on the sociopolitical context of women's lives, where individual problems are viewed as having societal and political roots. This perspective links the sexual abuse of children to the underlying social structure (e.g., Rush 1980). Sexual abuse is seen as a consequence of a patriarchal society in which there is an unequal power balance between men and women. Emphasizing that child sexual abuse is primarily perpetrated by males (Finkelhor & Russell 1984), feminist theorists argue that it is essential to view power and sex role socialization as key factors in child sexual abuse (Finkelhor 1984; Herman 1981; Rush 1980; Russell 1975, 1984). Child sexual abuse becomes one of many ways men abuse power. This model advocates for change in social structures and gender norms in order to stop abusive behaviour. The feminist model provides the only explanation of the gendered nature of the problem and thus is a critical lens through which to view child sexual abuse.

Other theoretical approaches locate the "cause" of sexual abuse at different, more micro-, levels. For example, some theories focus on the dysfunctional dynamics in certain families that create the conditions for sexual abuse. These family systems-oriented models identify characteristics that are commonly associated with sexual abuse, such as enmeshed boundaries within the family, unclear roles, isolation from community supports, avoidance of emotional expression and marital difficulties (Crosson-Tower 1999). Family systems theories have been criticized for implying that all family members share in the development of these dynamics and for ignoring the powerless position of women and children in families and society.

Other theories focus on individual pathology to explain why particular individuals perpetrate sexual abuse. For example, Marshall and Marshall (2000) suggest that the origins of sexual offending lie in offenders' childhood experiences of poor-quality relationships with their parents. Other models identify characteristics of offenders, such as low self-esteem, feelings of inadequacy, poor impulse control and lack of empathy, that are frequently associated with sexual abuse (Jenkins 1990). Social learning theories postulate that abuse is the result of behaviour which is learned and reinforced through modelling and is thus passed along from generation to generation. While these models may provide some insight into the occurrence of sexual abuse, they fail to acknowledge the social context in which abuse occurs.

Only a few theories attempt to integrate explanatory factors at various levels in an attempt to provide a more comprehensive theoretical explanation for the occurrence of child sexual abuse. For example, Finkelhor (1986b) describes four preconditions that must exist before sexual abuse can occur. The perpetrator must: (a) have some motivation to sexually abuse a child, (b) overcome internal inhibitions against acting on that motivation, (c) overcome external barriers to acting on that motivation and (d) overcome the child's resistance to sexual abuse. This model includes family patterns that contribute to sexual abuse as well as sociocultural factors which create a context in which sexual abuse can occur. Trepper and Barrett (1989) have also developed an integrated theory, the Multiple Systems Model, that examines socioenvironmental, family systems, individual personality/psychopathology and family of origin factors that create vulnerability within the family. Despite the usefulness of these models, there is not yet a dominant theory that integrates what is currently known about sexual abuse and moves those in the field to consensus about why sexual abuse occurs.

As we struggle to understand child sexual abuse, there is concurrent pressure to respond to the problem. As is always the case when dealing with social problems, we cannot suspend intervention until research and theory in the area have evolved to a place where direction for intervention is clear. Rather, intervention efforts and theory development occur as simultaneous, and often parallel, processes. The problem of child sexual abuse is no exception. Despite the limitations of existing theory, intervention must address a variety of issues, including: (a) ensuring the safety of the victims, (b) ameliorating the negative effects of the abuse on victims, (c) responding to the offenders' behaviours, (d) working with offenders in hopes of reducing the risk that further abuse will occur, (e) addressing the needs of the "secondary" victims of the abuse (non-offending parents, siblings, etc.) and (f) developing programs that ultimately prevent this form of violence. To accomplish such diverse goals, a range of interventions has been developed. These interventions involve multiple social systems (including the child welfare system, the criminal justice system and the mental health system) and practitioners with various skills and service mandates who fulfill divergent roles. In addition, addressing the issue of prevention requires thinking about extensive social change. Although at times the various interventions may appear to operate independently, they are each integral to our response to child sexual abuse. They are like pieces of a puzzle that fit together with the hope of forming a complete and comprehensive response to the problem.

As researchers and practitioners who confront the complexity of child sexual abuse, it is clear that there is much work to be done. While our knowledge about the causes of child sexual abuse and ideas about what constitutes effective intervention have increased, we still have much to do to significantly reduce the incidence of child sexual abuse, to effectively treat the devastating impact of abuse on its child victims, to adequately support non-offending mothers in their efforts to cope and to satisfactorily treat offenders to prevent further offences.

This volume, a collection of perspectives and strategies authored by Canadian researchers and practitioners, aims to advance our understanding of child sexual abuse by describing current research and intervention efforts and by identifying issues requiring further research and practice attention. Each chapter includes a review of the relevant literature, a description of the current work of the author(s) in the area of child sexual abuse and a discussion of implications for both practitioners and researchers. While each chapter is distinct by reflecting the specialized work within the expertise of the author(s), each contribution supports the premise that we must combine our collective knowledge and work together if we are to make a difference in the resolution of the problem of child sexual abuse. Without this sharing and collaboration, our ability to effectively address the challenges of child sexual abuse is seriously compromised.

The volume begins with this theme, emphasizing the interrelationship between many of the components of intervention in child sexual abuse. Burnside and Wilson provide an examination of the theoretical and practical issues associated with a family systems approach to intervention, highlighting the experience of the Family Sexual Abuse Treatment Program in Regina, Saskatchewan. This voluntary program, based in a child welfare agency, provides coordinated treatment to child and adolescent victims, non-offending parents, siblings and adolescent and adult offenders, employing a variety of treatment modalities. While the complexities of delivering comprehensive therapeutic services to all family members affected by intrafamilial sexual abuse are discussed, the necessity of considering the familial context in intervention is emphasized.

For some time, researchers and practitioners have speculated about the role of mothers in sexual abuse, resulting in many negative conclusions about mothers. In the second chapter of this volume, Hiebert-Murphy and Burnside critically examine the theoretical assumptions that have been made about mothers of children who have been sexually abused and challenge these assumptions by reviewing the findings of current research. They argue that a stress-coping framework provides an alternative perspective that can be useful for directing practice and research. This framework proposes that mothers' responses to sexual abuse disclosures be seen as their best attempts to cope in challenging situations. Ways in which practitioners can intervene to facilitate coping and implications for future research are discussed.

The third chapter offers a discussion of the range of therapeutic modalities used to address the negative effects of sexual abuse on children. As noted above, the emotional and behavioural consequences of sexual abuse can be debilitating for children, and timely, appropriate treatment can be helpful in mitigating these effects. Integrating their work on group therapy, De Luca and Grayston review in detail literature on the effectiveness of individual therapy (including play therapy and cognitive behavioural therapy), group therapy and family therapy with girls and boys who have been victims of sexual abuse. Their findings suggest that, while there is increasing evidence that individual, group and family therapies can be effective treatments for children who have been victimized, much more research is needed for us to fully understand the best ways to intervene.

An integrated understanding of child sexual abuse would be incomplete without a consideration of offenders. In the fourth chapter, Kreklewetz describes a study of incarcerated paternal incest offenders at a Canadian minimum security prison, which explored grooming patterns they employ with their immediate family members that are instrumental in their sexual offending. This study indicates that father-daughter incest is a deliberately planned process involving various contact and non-contact behaviours, and demonstrates that social factors influence the attitudes and perceptions of offenders. Kreklewetz explores how this information can be used in the assessment and treatment of incest offenders and discusses the implications for primary prevention efforts and treatment with non-offending parents and child victims.

Child sexual abuse has been defined as a criminal act, thus including a legal process as a component of intervention. In Manitoba, this has involved the establishment of a specialized family violence court. In the fifth chapter, Ursel and Gorkoff present the results of a study of child sexual abuse cases processed by the Family Violence Court between 1992 and 1997. Characteristics of these cases are examined, case outcomes are reviewed and the implications for child victims/witnesses and professionals within the justice system are identified. Ursel and Gorkoff argue that such descriptive research on the prosecution of child abuse cases is needed to inform decision making in regard to criminal justice intervention.

Although the majority of sexual assaults on children are committed by someone known to the child, there are some offenders who have no prior relationship with a child victim. The effect of such sexual abuse on children is also devastating, and therefore the topic warrants some attention in this volume. Additionally, due to society's reluctance to acknowledge the extent of intrafamilial sexual abuse, much of the prevention movement has focused on protecting children from assaults by strangers (Bagley 1991b). The final chapter examines the role of community notification programs in alerting communities to the identity of a known sexual offender who is considered at high risk to re-offend. Although it is a popular prevention strategy in many communities, little research has been conducted to assess the effectiveness of the community notification strategy. This chapter describes Sutherland's study of parents' responses to the concept of community notification, which utilized a simulation process to explore the range of reactions expressed by participants. Issues that need to be considered in the use of community notification programs are identified, and implications for policy and practice are discussed.

Overall, the collection of chapters contained in this volume provides a variety of perspectives on the complex problem of child sexual abuse. The contributors provide an update on various aspects of the issue, featuring their own experiences in research and practice, and suggest new directions for future intervention, prevention and research. While each chapter offers a distinct contribution to a more comprehensive understanding of the problem, the volume models the importance of generating multiple perspectives and working together to face the challenges of child sexual abuse. We must not become complacent about the progress we have made to date; nor should we feel overwhelmed by what still needs to be done. The devastating and staggering impact of child sexual abuse on families, on society and most importantly, on children, must continue to be acknowledged and must motivate us to work collaboratively towards a better understanding of the "pieces of the puzzle" of child sexual abuse.

Chapter 1

Connecting the Pieces

The Experience of the Family Sexual Abuse Treatment Program

Linda Burnside and D. Kim Wilson

Intrafamilial child sexual abuse is a complex social issue that challenges practitioners and researchers alike. In this relatively new field of research and intervention, many studies have focused on the various components of the problem or particular factors related to the abuse. For example, the characteristics of specific client groups, such as the child victims, may be examined, or a range of treatment modalities and interventions offered by practitioners, with varying areas of expertise or mandates from their social service agencies, may be evaluated. (These might include therapeutic services offered to child victims or counselling to sexual offenders.) However, much of the literature on intrafamilial child sexual abuse supports the premise that these components of child sexual abuse are interrelated. Therefore, a treatment approach with an ecological, family systems perspective that attends to the various components is crucial. This chapter reviews the literature concerning this theme and describes the approach of the Family Sexual Abuse Treatment Program of Saskatchewan Social Services in addressing child sexual abuse within an ecological, familial context.

Review of the Literature

The family systems approach purports that individuals are best understood within the context of relationships and interactions within the entire family (Corey 2001), asserting that the problem experienced by the individual can be viewed as a symptom of how the family system is functioning. In many respects, the revolutionary ideas of the family systems model, together with the feminist movement, facilitated the professional identification of the problem of intrafamilial sexual abuse (Finkelhor 1986b). The feminist perspective in particular is credited with identifying the fact that disturbing behaviours of children may be the result of sexual abuse within the family. As well, it challenged the traditional psychoanalytic view of incest, which essentially denied and minimized its occurrence. Family systems models provided language to practitioners to conceptualize family dynamics, such as boundaries, enmeshment, secrecy, disengagement, denial and roles—terms that are significant in understanding child sexual abuse within the family (Finkelhor 1986b; Sgroi 1982b; Trepper & Barrett 1989).

A number of studies confirm that many individual and family problems, including addictions and substance abuse, depressive disorders, suicidal behaviours, eating disorders, teenage pregnancies, post-traumatic stress and interpersonal difficulties, may have their origins in child sexual abuse (Briere & Elliot 1994; Carlson, Furby, Armstrong & Shlaes 1997). Research has also explored how some aspects of family life may constitute risk factors for intrafamilial sexual abuse: these include intergenerational experiences of abuse (Faller 1989), marital dissatisfaction, distance and conflict in the mother-daughter relationship, and violence between marital partners (Bagley & King 1990), parental substance abuse (Shah, Dail & Heinrichs 1995) and certain aspects of family structure (Shah et al. 1995). These studies suggest that, especially without intervention, sexual abuse can create symptoms that impair the functioning of the individual and that may increase the likelihood of the perpetration of abuse by the victim, either as an offender or as a non-offending partner (Lépine 1990).

However, the family systems approach has been the subject of criticism because of its limitations in the conceptualization of child sexual abuse. The family systems perspective sees intrafamilial sexual abuse as the product of a problematic family system, which implies that all family members share in the cause and the maintenance of the incest (Trepper & Barrett 1989). Despite the valuable contributions of the family systems model, this approach may lead to the unacceptable message that all family members share an equal responsibility for the abuse; it may therefore add to the child's feelings of guilt, promote mother blaming and fail to provide sufficient protection for the child. Additionally, it fails to place the family dynamics that contribute to the abuse in the larger societal context which allows incestuous behaviour to occur. Finally, the family systems approach may ignore, or minimize, the individual psychopathology of the offender, reducing his responsibility for his deviant behaviour and undermining the efficacy of treatment for the whole family (Finkelhor 1986b; Trepper & Barrett 1989).

An alternative model, proposed by Trepper and Barrett (1989), is more ecological in its orientation, acknowledging that there are many social systems that affect family members with regard to intrafamilial sexual abuse. These systems include cultural systems, family-of-origin systems, current family systems and individual psychological systems. An ecological model emphasizes the interactions of multiple factors, not only in understanding the origins of sexual abuse within the family, but in delivering the intervention and treatment services that are necessary to address the problem. Trepper and Barrett's (1989) family-based treatment program employs a variety of treatment techniques and modalities, including individual, family, marital, sibling and group therapy. While recognizing that individual therapy and group counselling are common, and often effective, treatment strategies in working with child victims of sexual abuse, non-offending mothers and offenders (Becker 1994; James & Nasjleti 1983; Johnson 1992; Monahon 1993; Sgroi 1982b), Trepper and Barrett (1989) view these approaches to therapy as a means to augment a family-based program, rather than to replace it. It is within family-oriented sessions, including marital therapy and sibling counselling, that the interactional patterns among family members can be most effectively assessed and altered.

There appears to be considerable support for the inclusion of family members in the treatment of sexual abuse (Bentovim & Ratner 1991; Berliner 1997; Deblinger & Heflin 1996; DiGiorgio-Miller 1998; Gil 1996; Johnson 1992; Melnechuk 1988). The literature contains descriptions of several family treatment approaches that include various interventions for child victims and other family members (e.g., Anderson & Mayes 1982; De Maio 1995; Giarretto 1981). These family-oriented treatment models are differentiated according to who participates in therapy and what themes are emphasized. Therapy is available to more than one member of the family, concurrently or collectively. Treatment modalities can include individual counselling (to facilitate self-expression, provide emotional validation and prepare the individual for relational work), group work (to increase self-awareness and create social support and an environment which promotes change), and family therapy (involving work with dyads, subsystems and/or the entire family). It should be emphasized that family-based intervention does not necessarily involve the offender. The offender is only included if he has accepted responsibility for the offending, if he makes significant gains towards altering his abusive behaviour and reducing his risk for reoffending and if it is the desire of the non-offending mother and children to maintain a relationship with him. Safety for the child is of primary importance in making decisions about who is included in the treatment and when particular interventions are appropriate.

An alternative strategy for involving families in intervention in cases of abuse is family group decision making. This intervention is based on the premise that halting abuse requires the collaboration of families, communities and public authorities (Burford & Pennell 1995; Connors & Oates 1997). The approach involves members of the immediate family in which abuse has occurred, extended kin, selected members from the family's social support network and professionals from the various disciplines (child welfare, police, justice, corrections, etc.) that are mandated to respond to the incidence of abuse. The intent is to assist family members to develop their own plans to deal with the incidence of abuse and to mobilize the assistance of formal helpers in implementing these plans. This approach has been successfully utilized to reduce the conflict that often develops between the family and the professionals, to decrease the risk of children being placed in alternative care and to refocus all parties on ensuring the safety of the victim and other children in the family.

While the advantages of employing a family-oriented perspective in the assessment and treatment of child sexual abuse are well documented, it can be challenging to coordinate the participation of the many disciplines and practitioners. Crucial to the coordination of roles and responsibilities is the involvement of the child protection agency. As noted by MacDonald, Levine, Adkins, Trute, Shannon and deLucia (1996), the child welfare system is legislated to ensure the safety of children and to make decisions regarding the reunification of families who have a history of abuse, incorporating the family's progress in therapy into case decisions. A variety of factors may complicate the working relationships between child welfare systems and providers of therapeutic interventions with the family. These include the involuntary and sometimes adversarial nature of child protection investigations (MacDonald et al. 1996), the inexperience and lack of training of child welfare workers in conducting family assessments (MacKinnon 1998), lack of clarity in goals of treatment between the child welfare system and the external therapist (Carl & Jurkovic 1983), preconceptions on the part of therapists about child abuse as a pathology and dysfunction not easily amenable to treatment (MacKinnon 1998) and the complexities of working in a multidisciplinary context (Gil 1996; Imber-Black 1988).

In some instances, formal working relationships between organizations have been utilized in the coordination and provision of intrafamilial sexual abuse intervention and treatment services, and such arrangements have the potential to mitigate some of the difficulties noted above. One example is the Sexual Abuse Treatment Program, a joint treatment initiative created in 1989 involving Knowles Centre, a residential treatment facility, and a local community child welfare agency, now a part of the larger Winnipeg Child and Family Services child welfare system (Chapman-Smyth 1993). Child and adolescent victims of intrafamilial sexual abuse were provided with individual therapy (by a therapist from Knowles Centre) and group treatment (provided by therapists from the child welfare agency) to address the effects of sexual abuse. While challenges were certainly encountered in this interagency approach, cooperation between the therapists of the two agencies facilitated better coordination of treatment services for family members and resulted in improved communication with the child protection workers and more collaborative case planning.

The Manitoba Rural Child Sexual Abuse Project endeavoured to provide a coordinated community service approach to intrafamilial child sexual abuse (Trute, Adkins & MacDonald 1994). This project involved a multi-agency team that included, among others, the child welfare agency, police, community mental health, the women's shelter and corrections. It aimed to ensure a smooth transition for families from the child welfare investigation through comprehensive treatment interventions. Extensive and sequential treatment plans, appropriate to the circumstances of each case, were developed and implemented. One of the unique characteristics of this project, which facilitated the process, was the provision of early crisis intervention services offered to the non-offending mother shortly after the child's disclosure. The evaluation of the project indicated that coordinated services help families to recover more quickly from the trauma associated with child sexual abuse.

Despite the apparent advantages of addressing child sexual abuse within a familial context, relatively few agencies in Canada have developed comprehensive family-based programs. This may be a reflection of the challenges inherent in this kind of programming as well as the extensive agency resources such treatment programs demand. This chapter describes how one program, the Family Sexual Abuse Treatment Program, successfully employs a family-based model within the multi-disciplinary environment of a child welfare agency. The experiences of this program may be helpful to other agencies interested in developing an ecological, family-based treatment program.

The Family Sexual Abuse Treatment Program

The Family Sexual Abuse Treatment Program (FSATP) of Saskatchewan Social Services in Regina, Saskatchewan, is an example of how one agency offers treatment services to families affected by intrafamilial child sexual abuse, both within the family context and in the child protection process. The program was created in October 1990 on the premise that protection of children cannot be considered to be complete without treatment of the child and the family in order to ameliorate as much as possible the damaging impact of the sexual abuse. The intent of the program is to provide an integrated service, from disclosure through investigation, to treatment and, finally, to case closure, in a format that is easily accessible to children and their families. One of its unique strengths is the program's ability to offer treatment to all family members: child victims, siblings, non-offending parents and adolescent or adult offenders.

The approach to treatment in the FSATP is essentially modelled after the work of Anderson and Mayes (1982). The program endeavours to follow the practice principles of child protection while offering treatment within a family systems context. From a child protection standpoint, treatment services are based on the belief that the physical and emotional safety of the child is of primary importance. Steps to ensure safety include reporting the abuse to the police, supporting the criminal justice process in prosecuting offenders, separating victims from offenders (preferably by assisting the non-offending parent to care for the child victim, with the offender out of the home) and encouraging offenders to participate in treatment (Fischer & Tchang 1994). The treatment program views the family as an organized collection of individuals, with each member having particular treatment needs that must be sufficiently addressed prior to the commencement of family therapy. This is balanced with the recognition that families also function in familiar relational patterns that may be altered by change and growth in one member of the family system.

The program is physically located apart from the main social services regional office to provide a sense of distance from the mandated child protection role and to facilitate access to therapy sessions after regular working hours. However, the therapists in the program are all employees of Saskatchewan Social Services, the provincial department mandated to provide child protection services. The program is staffed by three therapists and a supervisor. As well, child protection workers, youth facility workers and practicum students from programs of social work, registered nursing and psychiatric nursing have often assisted in co-leading treatment groups. Treatment modalities include individual counselling, dyadic sessions, family therapy and group therapy. Play and art therapy are also available for children and have been found to be effective with adolescent and adult clients as well.

While the program is voluntary, referrals of families are made by child protection staff, who first ensure that the safety of the child has been addressed and that all provincial protocols with regard to child abuse investigations have been followed. Both the referral and an orientation session can occur soon after the child protection investigation is initiated. Following the referral, a therapist meets with those members who are appropriate for treatment to discuss their expectations of the program and to ensure that their participation is voluntary. In this session, the family is provided with information about what to expect in both the child protection and treatment processes: this allows the therapist to take advantage of the motivation for treatment that may decrease once the family moves out of the crisis stage and into the more defensive behaviour that typically marks the disclosure of sexual abuse. The child protection worker is often included in the orientation meeting in order to identify the safety issues that need to be addressed in treatment. Family members are advised of the cooperative and open relationship between the child protection worker and therapist and that the safety of the children is of primary importance in all treatment.

If the family agrees to become involved in the treatment program, the therapist engages family members in individual counselling, focusing on each person's identified treatment issues. Indicators of progress in individual therapy include the family member's ability to talk about the abuse, to understand his or her role in the family dynamics that created a context for the occurrence of the abuse and to acknowledge the offender's responsibility for the abuse. Once this aspect of individual treatment is sufficiently completed, the therapist can begin to engage family members in dyadic counselling, dealing with a different range of issues related to relationships between family members. When the therapist and family members feel that sufficient progress has been made in individual and dyadic therapy, counselling for the family (which may or may not include the offender) is offered. Family members are encouraged to attend treatment groups at any time while in therapy. Although this description of services sounds somewhat linear, it is important to note that in practice, therapists in the program have found that families progress through treatment in a variety of ways, depending on their readiness to address difficult issues or to manage particular treatment modalities. Frequently, families will leave treatment for a time period, until new issues or the stresses of unresolved issues compel them to resume therapy.

The program has found that a number of families intend to reunite as soon as the child protection concerns have been resolved and criminal court processes have been completed. Recognizing that reunification, with or without the offender, may be the family's choice, therapists of the program have found it helpful to ensure that family sessions are part of the treatment plan. Approximately half of all families have made use of family counselling sessions. The focus of these sessions is on relationships between individual family members within the family unit; the goal is to establish healthy family rules, roles, boundaries and communication. Issues discussed in the family sessions may include factors or events that precipitated the abuse, supervision and child care issues, family boundaries (such as respecting individual privacy and appropriate sleeping arrangements) and family secrets. The sessions provide a forum for victims to practise some of the skills they have developed in individual and group counselling. The non-offending parent is encouraged to express her support for the child in these sessions and assisted to hear her child's feelings and needs. If the offender has accepted responsibility for the abuse and is included in family sessions, a safe environment is established for the child to talk about the impact of the abuse and the range of feelings experienced. Family members are encouraged to discuss the vision they have for their family in the future.

Family sessions provide the therapist with information which is important in assessing the level of family functioning and prognosis for reunification. This information is shared with child protection workers to help them estimate the risk of further abuse and the need for ongoing child welfare involvement. In these sessions families can seek feedback from the therapist about their progress and decisions and may determine potential support services in the community to assist them in healthy functioning after the conclusion of therapy.

For more than a decade, the FSATP has been meeting the needs of many families and child protection workers. Still, the program faces some challenges. Resources and funding are limited, which sometimes results in delays before families can begin treatment. Professional disagreements between the child protection worker and therapist occur on occasion. High workloads and the different worksites of protection workers and therapists can impede communication. Sometimes protection workers hold unrealistic expectations of the program, such as the assumption that therapists will solicit further disclosures from child victims. Strategies to address these difficulties, such as regular meetings, frequent communication between meetings and role clarification, are crucial components of a collaborative team intervention and an effective treatment plan for the family.

Overall, the benefits have been found to outweigh the obstacles. The FSATP provides an accessible treatment resource to both families and child protection services. The capacity of the program to respond to referrals in the early stages of the child protection investigation enhances the effectiveness of the therapy. The close coordination between the child welfare and therapeutic services facilitates a comprehensive response to families affected by sexual abuse.

Experiences of Clients in the Family Sexual Abuse Treatment Program

Often, the most powerful and poignant illustrations of the effectiveness of treatment services come from the experiences of clients in treatment. While these anecdotes and stories cannot be compared in statistical terms, they add a compelling and human perspective to be considered by practitioners, researchers and policy-makers in the development and implementation of treatment policies and programs. There are many examples of these experiences from clients of the Family Sexual Abuse Treatment Program, some of which are noted here.

Participants of an adolescent girls treatment group chose to make a video for child protection workers and police officers, offering advice on how to work more effectively with sexually abused adolescents. The adolescents recounted how sexual abuse was like a "life sentence" in terms of its impact and that they felt that many professionals are unaware of the profound effects sexual abuse has on victims. They used the video to describe in their own words what it felt like not to be believed by family members and how difficult it was to have to move out of the home because of the offender's actions. Although the video has been used on a limited basis to protect the confidentiality of the group members, it proved to be a powerful exercise for them. In particular, most of the adolescents held negative perceptions of their experiences with the child protection and justice systems, and found the creation of the video an empowering way to process their experiences and influence the response of professionals in the system.

After discussing their many difficult experiences with the courts and dealing with the charges facing their offenders after sexual abuse, members of an adolescent girls group arranged for a "Justice Day." Various professionals from the criminal justice system, including a police officer, domestic violence counsellor, prosecutor and judge, were invited to meet with the group members for a day of sharing. The professional guests described the justice process according to their perspectives and roles in the system, helping the adolescents understand the principles of justice. More importantly, the group members shared their perspectives of justice in a very personal way: based on their experiences, many girls saw the police and prosecutors as "good" in supporting their disclosures of abuse, but described the defence lawyers and judges as "bad," as they appeared to believe the offender and not the child. The girls indicated that they learned a great deal about the workings of the criminal justice system from their "Justice Day." The invited professionals stated that they learned a great deal about the impact of sexual abuse and of the justice system on adolescents. One of the professionals was moved enough to disclose a childhood history of sexual abuse to the group.

In consultation with her therapist and the program's group facilitators, one non-offending mother, an adult survivor of sexual abuse, spoke to several of the girls' groups about her experience of being sexually abused, particularly about the physical symptoms that continued to manifest themselves as "body memories" in her adulthood. For example, she described how the smell of a particular brand of after-shave continues to bring on dissociation symptoms and that she is still bothered by sore knees and nausea after encountering the scent. The sharing of personal stories helped to validate the experiences of the group participants, who experienced similar symptoms, and allowed the non-offending mother to utilize her traumatic memories in a constructive, and therefore healing, way.

Family sessions have also provided powerful opportunities for change. In one such session, the therapist used a genogram to assist a non-offending mother and her three children to understand how family patterns had contributed to a reoccurrence of sexual abuse throughout several generations. The mother took a felt marker and drew a line underneath the genogram symbols representing her children and emphasized to her children that the cycle of abuse would end there. The undeniable message conveyed by this action to her children was her understanding of their trauma and her total commitment to their safety. It was a compelling metaphor for this family's progress in treatment.

Finally, an adolescent offender who participated in the program had this sobering thought on why some children who were sexually abused might become sexual offenders: "They want to pass on the pain." A youth with difficulties in maintaining physical boundaries with others, including with the therapist, he seemed unable to control himself from repeating the boundary violations he had experienced as a child. Real progress in therapy was evident when he began to respect the physical boundaries of others without being prompted or cautioned. Clearly, without treatment intervention, the likelihood of the pain being perpetuated in ongoing sexual abuse, as well as in other debilitating symptoms, is evident.

Evaluation of the Family Sexual Abuse Treatment Program
A formal evaluation of the FSATP was conducted from 1990 to 1994 (Fischer & Tchang 1994) to identify the demographics of families accessing the program and to assess progress of family members in treatment. The results of the evaluation indicated that 88 percent of child victims referred to the program received individual therapy, 26 percent received both individual and group therapy, and 12 percent participated only in group counselling. Non-offending mothers who were referred to the treatment program participated in individual therapy in 73 percent of families and in group counselling in 21 percent of cases. Of the sexual offenders who were members of the families referred to the program, 27 percent received individual therapy, and 15 percent participated in group therapy, indicating that many offenders did not participate in any treatment through the FSATP. It was noted that the majority of offenders who agreed to participate in therapy were adolescents and that adult offenders tended not to participate in treatment at all unless mandated by the courts.

A variety of standardized measures were utilized during the evaluation period to assess therapeutic progress in treatment (see Fischer & Tchang 1994 for a detailed description of program outcomes). To summarize, the evaluation demonstrated that clients of the program made some encouraging gains in treatment. For children, improvements in functioning were noted in reduced levels of anxiety and depression, a decreased incidence of delinquent behaviours and improved ability to express emotions. Children also demonstrated somewhat higher levels of trust during therapy and were less likely to deny or minimize their sexual abuse. Group therapy was found to be particularly valuable in assisting victims to develop stronger peer relationships and social supports. However, children continued to blame themselves for the abuse to a great extent and continued to experience strong feelings of anger and hostility toward the offender, and often toward the non-offending parent.

Non-offending parents, who often presented with high levels of anxiety, depression and dysphoria at the time of referral, did not demonstrate significantly measurable clinical change in some areas, but, during the course of treatment, did attribute less responsibility for the abuse to the child and were more able to empathize with the child victim. Many of these women lacked social supports and appropriate peer relationships; this social isolation was identified as a major contributor to such dysfunctional family relationships as the tendency for non-offending mothers to have sibling-like relationships with their children and poor communication and blurred role boundaries with the offenders. These family dynamics are considered to be risk factors for the occurrence of sexual abuse and did not change markedly for these clients during treatment. Fischer and Tchang (1994: 187) conclude that treatment for non-offending mothers must therefore be directed toward addressing these issues, maintaining that "mothers, perhaps more than anyone, are able to restore family functioning to normal" through their improved ability to communicate and model appropriate role boundaries. However true, such a conclusion can be misinterpreted as mother-blaming. It is imperative to note that 81 percent of non-offending mothers were themselves survivors of childhood sexual abuse, and 70 percent had not received treatment for their childhood victimization. It is, therefore, quite possible that these non-offending mothers were facing a multitude of challenges, in addition to the stresses of dealing with the sexual abuse of one's child, that affected their ability to derive more significant therapeutic gain from treatment. This interpretation is consistent with the findings of Corcoran (1998).

Treatment outcomes were available for only a small number of offenders, as few participated in the FSATP. Results suggested that treatment promotes some improvement in positive affect and self-control for adolescent offenders and generates greater empathy and understanding on the part of offenders for child victims. However, there was no change in acceptance of responsibility for the sexual abuse during therapy. Offenders continued to blame victims to a large extent and non-offending parents to a lesser extent for the occurrence of sexual abuse. Stereotypical gender attitudes, favouring males and objectifying females, also did not change in treatment: this outcome was considered to be a result of socialization factors that contributed to the tendency of offenders to equate sexual abuse with power. Additionally, 63 percent of the sexual offenders who participated in the program disclosed past sexual victimization; 64 percent of these offenders revealed they had received no treatment for their childhood abuse. The existence of these past, unresolved traumas may have inhibited the efficacy of treatment for these offenders.

One of the limitations of the evaluation is that clients receiving dyadic or family sessions were not incorporated into the study, although these services were provided by the program. Fischer and Tchang (1994) stated that a number of family relationship issues, such as family roles and boundaries, interpersonal communication, conflict resolution and expression of emotions, remained unaddressed and unresolved at the conclusion of individual and group treatment. While individual and group therapy can deal with these issues to some extent, the authors assert that family-oriented therapy is required to assist families in adequately resolving these issues and achieving effective family functioning. Furthermore, they suggest that such therapeutic outcome is likely a long-term process for most families, in the range of three to five years from the beginning of individual treatment to the conclusion of family therapy.

Even with this limitation, the evaluation of the FSATP facilitates our understanding of the need to involve family members in dyadic, subsystem and family counselling sessions. Therapy for victims alone is clearly not sufficient to resolve all of the child's issues; nor does it adequately address the relationship issues between the child and other family members. Concurrent treatment for child victims, non-offending parents and offenders furthers therapeutic gains for families who have experienced intrafamilial sexual abuse, especially in terms of appropriate allocation of responsibility for the abuse and empathy for the child victim, but still does not attend to the family dynamics that set the environment in which the sexual abuse occurred. The provision of family counselling for child victims with their non-offending parents and siblings, and, where appropriate and possible, with their offenders is strongly recommended.

Implications for Practice and Research

The clinical experience and evaluation findings of the FSATP point to the fundamental need for a family-oriented perspective with regard to intrafamilial child sexual abuse. Although individual and group therapy facilitates some degree of therapeutic gain, there remain significant relational issues that impede family functioning and contribute to the risk of intrafamilial sexual abuse and are therefore best addressed in a familial context. This conclusion is consistent with the findings of other researchers and practitioners who have found it beneficial and preferable to involve family members, at least to some extent, in treatment interventions toward the resolution of child sexual abuse (as summarized by Friedrich 1996, and as noted above). However, treatment efficacy studies that have demonstrated a relationship between specific treatment interventions and reduction of symptomology have often focused on a narrow range of symptoms (Friedrich 1996). In practice, a child typically presents a broader range of symptoms, suggesting that a range of treatment modalities may be appropriate and, in fact, necessary (Shah et al. 1995; Trepper & Barrett 1989). Certainly, research that seeks to enhance our understanding of the effectiveness of a family approach and that further clarifies its role and sequence in a multimodal comprehensive treatment strategy is required.

Length of treatment is an important consideration, raised by Fischer and Tchang (1994) in their evaluation of the FSATP and also explored by Friedrich (1996). Family members affected by intrafamilial child sexual abuse frequently experience a multitude of significant therapeutic issues that are not easily or quickly resolved, suggesting that comprehensive treatment for most families is a long-term process. Some, such as James and Nasjleti (1983) and Trepper and Barrett (1989), advise that treatment in a familial context can be expected to last approximately two years or more. Fischer and Tchang (1994) found that clients of the FSATP had many outstanding clinical issues after individual and group therapy, a process that had already involved up to thirty months of treatment. However, although some studies indicate that short-term therapy can produce certain results, identification of an optimal length of treatment is not yet established (Friedrich 1996).

Since resolution of intrafamilial child sexual abuse is often a lengthy process, an important practice dilemma is the ability of agency treatment programs and private therapists to meet the needs of all clients. Organizational funding constraints, high demands for services, competing agency priorities and the inability of clients to pay for therapy themselves all contribute to limited treatment opportunities for families in need. If effective therapy truly is a long-term investment for both clients and practitioners, then delays in receiving necessary treatment will be inevitable. A major challenge for agency practitioners and private therapists alike is to balance the need for clients to receive "enough" therapy with the need to ensure that treatment is readily available to all who require it.

Central to the question of length of treatment is the acknowledgement that most communities have limited treatment resources to offer. Providing adequate treatment is a complex, time-consuming, resource-intensive and therefore expensive undertaking for most organizations (Bagley 1985). Additionally, when social service agencies are facing high demands for service and government pressure to reduce expenditures, cuts in service are often in the area of treatment (Crosson-Tower 1999). While fiscal responsibility is an appropriate expectation of agencies, the extensive treatment needs of families affected by sexual abuse should also be an adequately funded priority of governments and other program supporters. All child victims, as well as their family members, should have access to a full range of treatment resources, which requires the support and expansion of existing services, as well as the development of additional services in our communities (Rogers 1992).

Another area deserving further research, as identified by Fischer and Tchang (1994), is related to the long-term outcomes of treatment and the need to determine the extent to which treatment effects are maintained over time. It is assumed that much of the current research with adult survivors of sexual abuse involves clients who likely did not receive any form of treatment in childhood. While this research helps to describe the range and intensity of traumatic symptoms for victims of intrafamilial sexual abuse, it does not facilitate our understanding of how individual, group and family therapy might mitigate these symptoms over time. The authors recommend the use of longitudinal studies to assess the stability of treatment outcomes for family members, particularly for child victims, who would need to be monitored for a number of years after the conclusion of therapy to fully evaluate this theme.

The experiences of the FSATP, as well as others such as the Manitoba Rural Child Sexual Abuse Project (Trute et al. 1994), highlight the value of early intervention in intrafamilial child sexual abuse as a means to more readily engage all family members in treatment. A number of factors, however, create barriers to early intervention. These include the funding and service issues identified above that result in waiting lists and limited treatment opportunities, as well as the lengthy judicial processes in child sexual abuse cases, which often interfere with the commencement and progress of therapy. This is especially true in providing treatment to sexual offenders, who are less likely to participate in therapy until mandated by the courts. The characteristics of the disclosure crisis (such as the threat to family stability and the psychological impact of trauma) also can prevent families from seeking treatment services at a time when they would most benefit from supportive intervention (Trute et al. 1994). Strategies to mitigate these barriers are warranted and require the assistance of researchers, the innovations of policy-makers and the creativity of social service organizations in developing approaches, in partnership with other systems (child protection, justice, victim advocacy, etc.), that will best facilitate access to treatment for families.

Difficulties in the coordination of services, particularly between child welfare agencies and treatment providers, can also be a barrier to early intervention (MacKinnon 1998; Trute et al. 1994). One of the remedies undertaken by the FSATP to confront this particular obstacle involves the delivery of treatment services by a program within the child welfare system. This approach allows for closer collaboration between child welfare workers and therapists and facilitates coordi- nated case planning to address both safety issues and treatment inter- ventions. The importance of cooperative working relationships be- tween child welfare systems and treatment providers is well-docu- mented (De Maio 1995; Gil 1996; James & Nasjleti 1983; MacKinnon 1998; Melnechuk 1988; Trute et al. 1994). However, some families ex- press distrust of the child welfare system and resent the intrusive actions that mandated intervention often requires. This factor may have implications for acceptance of treatment within a child welfare environment. There is a need to more fully examine the advantages and disadvantages of a treatment service that is fully integrated within a child protection department.

It is evident that there is still considerable work to do in under- standing how to better connect all the pieces in providing treatment for intrafamilial child sexual abuse. In light of the challenges described above, some communities are beginning to advocate for innovative intervention and treatment models, such as the variations of family group decision making described by Burford and Pennell (1995) and Connors and Oates (1997). Such multidisciplinary team initiatives in- clude features of treatment in a familial context, such as active involve- ment of all family members in the process; they also encourage of- fender responsibility and participation in treatment as appropriate alternatives to criminal proceedings. These models, developed within First Nations communities, have not been widely used in urban set- tings with either Aboriginal or non-Aboriginal families, but warrant further exploration.

What is clear from the experience of the Family Sexual Abuse Treatment Program is that the pieces are interrelated. Victims, non- offending parents and offenders are part of a complex, dynamic family system; isolating their treatment issues limits the efficacy of therapy to some extent, as relationship patterns that contribute to the occurrence of sexual abuse are not sufficiently challenged and altered. The pro- gram has shown that it is possible and beneficial to coordinate therapy for all family members within one treatment service. Additionally, the program demonstrates the potential for child welfare systems and therapeutic services to work together in a collaborative fashion toward a coordinated response to the multiple facets of child sexual abuse.

Chapter 2

It's Not Her Fault

A Stress-Coping Approach to Understanding Mothers of Children Who Have Been Sexually Abused

Diane Hiebert-Murphy and Linda Burnside

Introduction

The sexual abuse literature demonstrates considerable interest in mothers of children who have been sexually abused. In the early literature, clinicians often portrayed mothers negatively; for example, mothers were described as dependent (Zuelzer & Reposa 1983), infantile (Kaufman, Peck & Tagiuri 1954), passive (Raphling, Carpenter & Davis 1967), rejecting (Gordon 1955) and frigid (Justice & Justice 1979). Unfortunately the clinical concern for mothers far exceeded the empirical evidence; many writers based their conclusions on clinical experience or poorly controlled case studies (e.g., Cohen 1983; Guntheil & Avery 1977; Lustig, Dresser, Spellman & Murray 1966; Weiner 1962; Zuelzer & Reposa 1983). It is only recently that mothers have been studied in a systematic way. A variety of approaches have been taken in the research, focusing, for example, on individual characteristics of mothers, on the emotional and behavioural responses of mothers following the sexual abuse disclosure and on understanding the context in which mothers attempt to deal with the disclosure. The purpose of this chapter is to provide an overview of these approaches and to discuss the ways in which a stress-coping model can be used to further our understanding of mothers.

Individual Characteristics of Mothers

Given the clinical descriptions of mothers previously noted, it is not surprising that researchers have attempted to determine if the personalities of mothers of children who have been sexually abused are "normal" and if there are differences between mothers of children who have been sexually abused and other mothers. Various studies have evaluated the personalities of mothers (Friedrich 1991; Groff 1987; Muram, Rosenthal & Beck 1994; Myer 1985; Peterson, Basta & Dykstra 1993; Scott & Stone 1986). These studies suggest that mothers vary considerably in personality. While some studies have found various differences between mothers of children who have been abused and mothers from control or comparison groups, they conclude that there is no evidence to suggest that mothers of children who have been sexually abused display severe personality disturbance.

There has also been considerable interest in examining prior abuse among mothers. Early research focused on the prevalence of sexual abuse among mothers in families in which incest occurred. These studies varied in their findings, reporting that between 20 percent and 65 percent of the mothers had themselves been victims of sexual abuse (Goodwin, McCarthy & DiVasto 1981; Melnechuk 1988; Myer 1985). In several studies involving mothers of children who were victims of either intrafamilial or extrafamilial abuse, between 28 percent and 74 percent reported that mothers had experienced sexual abuse (Deblinger, Stauffer & Landsberg 1994; Friedrich 1991; Hiebert-Murphy 1998). Several studies have found that women who had experienced sexual abuse had more difficulty coping with their children's disclosures than did women who had not themselves been sexually abused (Deblinger et al. 1994; Friedrich 1991; Hiebert-Murphy 1998; Timmons-Mitchell, Chandler-Holtz & Semple 1996).

Fewer studies have considered the effects of abuse by male partners on mothers, with the focus being the prevalence of such abuse. A number of studies have reported a high incidence of partner violence in families in which incest occurred (Browning & Boatman 1977; deYoung 1994; Dietz & Craft 1980; Julian & Mohr 1979; Melnechuk 1988; Tormes 1972; Truesdell, McNeil & Deschner 1986). Only a few studies have assessed domestic violence against mothers of children abused by partners, other relatives and non-relatives. For example, Deblinger, Hathaway, Lippman and Steer (1993) found that 57 percent of the women reported experiences of physical abuse by a partner. Hiebert-Murphy (2000b) found that 36 percent of the women in her sample were currently in a partner relationship in which they had experienced some type of abuse (physical or emotional). Twenty percent of the women experienced physical abuse in a current relationship and 65 percent of the women reported physical abuse in past relationships.

The focus on individual characteristics of mothers suggests that while there may be some differences between mothers of children who have been sexually abused and other mothers, they are not "abnormal," and thus individual psychopathology is not a useful theory to explain the behaviour of these women. There is evidence that many mothers have experienced prior abuse, although, given the state of current research, the role that these experiences play in the mother's reaction to the abuse must be interpreted cautiously. The absence of control groups in most studies makes it unclear if the prevalence of abuse among mothers of children who have been sexually abused is greater than expected or simply reflects prevalence rates in the general population. Furthermore, more research is needed to clearly establish a causal relationship between prior abuse and responses to the disclosure. Overall, while individual differences in this population may suggest factors that influence mothers' experiences, this approach is not likely to result in a sufficient explanation of the responses of mothers to sexual abuse disclosures.

Effects of Disclosure on Mothers

Research has also focused on the effects of the disclosure on mothers' behaviour and functioning. This research has looked at two major outcomes: emotional functioning of mothers following the disclosure and whether or not mothers are supportive of their children. Not surprisingly, clinical literature suggests that mothers experience distress following disclosure (e.g., Regehr 1990). Several reports indicate that some mothers experience significant difficulties following disclosure, including hospitalization for physical and / or emotional difficulties (De Jong 1986) and suicide attempts (Goodwin 1981). Numerous quantitative studies provide evidence that mothers experience distress following the disclosure of sexual abuse. Although it is not clear if this level of distress is different from the distress experienced by mothers whose children have other difficulties (Wagner 1991), there is evidence suggesting that mothers of sexually abused children experience greater distress than mothers of children who are not abused (Kelley 1990; Manion et al. 1996). These studies also suggest that there is variability in mothers' distress. Not all mothers experience clinically significant levels of distress (Newberger, Gremy, Waternaux & Newberger 1993). Several qualitative studies have confirmed that sexual abuse is distressing for mothers and affects their functioning (Carter 1993; Hooper 1992).

A frequent assumption is that mothers, although aware of the abuse, fail to act supportively towards their children. There are a number of studies that challenge this belief. These studies suggest that the stereotype of the collusive mother is not supported by data (e.g., De Jong 1988; deYoung 1994; Everson et al. 1989; Faller 1988; Johnson 1992; Mannarino & Cohen 1986; Pierce & Pierce 1985; Sirles & Franke 1989). While some mothers are non-supportive, the majority of mothers believe their children's accounts of abuse and respond in a protective manner. Based on these data, it seems most appropriate to view mothers as a heterogeneous group who have varying responses to the sexual abuse of their children. Although this research has challenged the mother-blaming tone of clinically based literature, it has not been informed by theory and has done little to further our theoretical conceptualizations of mothers.

The Context of Mothers' Lives

Another approach to research has been influenced by a feminist perspective which sees sexual abuse as connected to a social structure and social values that support inequality (e.g., Carter 1999; McIntyre 1981; Russell 1984; Wattenberg 1985). Feminist theorists argue that it is essential to view the unequal power distribution between men and women and sex role socialization as key factors in child sexual abuse (Finkelhor 1984; Herman 1981; Rush 1980; Russell 1975, 1984). They are particularly critical of the role that mothers are given in sexual abuse. According to Hooper (1992), women are given a disproportionate share of responsibility for the welfare of their children. Although expected to fulfill these parental responsibilities, women are not given the necessary power or resources (Hooper 1992; Myer 1985). When abuse occurs, as much emphasis is often placed on the failure of the non-offending mother to protect the child as on the abusive behaviour of the perpetrator (Elbow & Mayfield 1991). Mothers are seen as responsible for the abuse by failing to function in their roles as partner and/or mother. In some cases they are accused of colluding with the perpetrator, thereby allowing the abuse to continue. A feminist perspective rejects this "mother blaming" and asserts that mothers and the choices they make must be understood within the sociopolitical context in which these women live.

Building on these ideas, a growing number of studies have considered the impact of the social context on women's experiences (e.g., Carter 1993, 1999; Dempster 1992; Hooper 1992; Johnson 1992; Newton 1996) These qualitative studies look at the effects of disclosure on women and the role of external factors (including social institutions) in their attempts to understand mothers in the post-disclosure period. The findings suggest that disclosure has a traumatic impact on the psychological, social and economic functioning of mothers, that "mother blaming" continues to exist in policies and practices involved in intervention in child sexual abuse and that contextual factors such as financial power and sex role socialization are critical in understanding mothers' actions.

Conclusion

To date a variety of strategies have been taken in an attempt to increase our understanding of mothers of children who have been sexually abused. For the most part, researchers have endeavoured to identify factors that are important in distinguishing mothers of children who have been sexually abused from other women and that may shed light on the responses that women make to the disclosure. Few studies have been conceptualized within a theoretical framework (Tamraz 1996), speaking to the need for new models to explain the role of mothers in child sexual abuse (Joyce 1997). Furthermore, research has largely neglected to explore societal conditions that interfere with a mother's ability to protect her child (Corcoran 1998).

In her challenge of the mother-blaming tone of much of the sexual abuse literature, Hooper (1989) argues that mothers' responses are better understood as coping strategies than as collusion. According to her perspective, mothers' behaviours should be viewed as attempts to deal with the stressful situation and cope with their own needs and feelings, as well as the many other demands of the situation. Building on this idea, this chapter outlines the ways in which a stress-coping framework can contribute to the field by guiding research and identifying important practice issues.

Stress and Coping as Useful Constructs

The theoretical constructs of stress and coping have increasingly been used to understand the relationship between various life stressors and psychosocial outcomes for individuals. Historically the concept of stress has been studied in numerous ways and has had various meanings. While one view holds that stress is the individual's response to challenging events (e.g., Selye 1976), another view regards stress as events external to the individual that make demands on that individual (e.g., Holmes & Rahe 1967). Stress has also been treated as a transactional concept which suggests that whether or not experiences are stressful depends on the balance between demands and resources available to meet those demands (Lazarus & Launier 1978). Stress is experienced when the perceived demands (either external or internal) are appraised to exceed the individual's capability to meet those demands. Within this framework, the relationship between life events and functioning is mediated by coping processes (Moos & Billings 1982).

Coping is usually defined as the efforts made to master, tolerate or reduce demands that exceed the person's resources (Pearlin & Schooler 1978). There are many coping strategies, including active problem solving, cognitive avoidance and emotional discharge (for a review, see Moos & Billing 1982). Several efforts have been made to develop classification schemes for coping responses. For example, coping responses have been classified based on the focus of coping (Lazarus & Launier 1978; Pearlin & Schooler 1978) and on the method of coping (Billings & Moos 1981, 1984). Moos (1990) has developed an inventory which attempts to combine these two approaches to classification; this inventory divides coping responses into approach responses and avoidance responses (i.e., the focus of coping) and further divides each category into cognitive coping and behavioural coping (i.e., the method of coping).

There is much research indicating an association between coping strategies and adjustment in individuals exposed to stressful experiences (e.g., Billings & Moos 1981; Holahan & Moos 1986, 1987, 1991; Kessler, Price & Wortman 1985; Pearlin & Schooler 1978). The concept of coping has been useful in understanding the adjustment of mothers dealing with various challenges, such as seriously ill and hospitalized children (Barbarin & Chesler 1986; Wyckoff & Erickson 1987), single parenthood (Mednick 1987), children with disabilities (Friedrich 1979; Peterson 1984) and divorce (Propst, Pardington, Ostrom & Watkins 1986).

Given its demonstrated usefulness it seems reasonable to use a stress-coping framework to explore mothers' reactions to a disclosure of sexual abuse. Within this model, the disclosure of sexual abuse—a stressful event—places demands on a mother. The ways in which she responds to these demands (i.e., the coping responses that she makes) will be influenced by a variety of factors and will affect the outcome (e.g., her emotional adjustment). This stress-coping framework encourages the identification of factors that can account for differences in outcome. These factors can exist at the level of the individual, the family, the community and the society and thus are consistent with perspectives that emphasize the importance of context (e.g., a feminist perspective). The model provides a way to integrate research findings that suggest a relationship between various psychosocial factors and measures of outcome and also provides a theoretical explanation for these findings.

The concept of coping challenges much of the mother blaming in situations of child sexual abuse. Mothers' behaviours are reframed as their best efforts to deal with a difficult situation, thus shifting us away from a negative view of mothers. The choices mothers make are seen as constrained not just by their individual characteristics but also by the social and political context within which those choices for acting are made. This shift in viewpoint is consistent with a feminist view of women's lives and acknowledges the effect of context on women's actions.

Studies Using a Stress-Coping Model

Several studies have been undertaken to further our understanding of the coping of mothers of children who have been sexually abused. In one project (Hiebert-Murphy 1998, 2000a) a quantitative approach was taken to explore the relationship between coping responses and mothers' emotional functioning and between coping responses and their experiences of parenting. It was expected that these factors of adjustment would be affected by risk factors as well as stress-resistance factors.

One hundred and two women with children who had made disclosures of sexual abuse completed a variety of measures which assessed risk factors, stress-resistance factors and adjustment. Coping was assessed with a standardized measure of coping strategies, The Coping Responses Inventory (CRI) - Part II (Moos 1990). The CRI (Part II) is composed of eight subscales which measure two types of coping responses: approach and avoidance. Approach coping responses involve active attempts to deal with an event, including logical analysis, positive reappraisal, seeking support and information and taking problem-solving action. Avoidance strategies involve behavioural or cognitive efforts that avoid dealing with the event and include cognitive avoidance, acceptance or resignation, seeking alternative rewards and emotional discharge. For the purposes of this project, participants were asked to assess the strategies they had used to cope with the sexual abuse disclosure.

The findings of one study (Hiebert-Murphy 1998) indicated that mothers who had themselves experienced sexual abuse during childhood or adolescence reported greater emotional distress following their children's disclosures of sexual abuse than did women who did not have a history of sexual abuse. A lack of social support from friends and family and relying on avoidance coping strategies to deal with the disclosure were also related to greater emotional distress among mothers. As predicted by a stress-coping framework, the stress-resistance factors (social support and coping strategies) were important in understanding the women's emotional distress, even after controlling for the risk factor of child sexual abuse history.

A second study (Hiebert-Murphy 2000a) used a similar framework, although the outcome of interest was mothers' satisfaction with parenting and their sense of efficacy as parents. In this study child behaviour problems and maternal sexual abuse history were considered stressors while social support and coping strategies were explored as stress resistance factors. Child behaviour problems were found to be related to both parenting satisfaction and efficacy. The more conduct problems mothers reported observing in their children, the lower their satisfaction with parenting and their sense of efficacy as parents. The greater a child's sexual behaviour problems following the abuse, the lower was the mother's sense of efficacy as a parent. Maternal sexual abuse history was not related to either parenting satisfaction or efficacy. Although social support and coping strategies were not related to parenting efficacy, as expected, greater social support from friends and a reliance on approach coping strategies were associated with increased parenting satisfaction, even after controlling for the presence of child behaviour problems. The findings provide some support for the usefulness of looking at stressors and coping as a way to understand parenting satisfaction among mothers.

The quantitative approach to exploring coping among mothers, used in the abc ve studies, has a number of strengths. First of all, the use of a standardized measure of coping allows for this work to build on the large body of coping research previously done, using this or similar measures of coping. The validity of the measure, as evidenced by previous research, allows certain conclusions to be made about coping among this population. For example, an avoidance approach to coping is associated with poorer outcome. This conclusion has important implications for practitioners. While many factors which may influence outcome cannot be altered (e.g., factors related to the abuse, such as severity), coping responses are an appropriate target for intervention. Practitioners can work together with women to help them develop more active approaches to dealing with child sexual abuse, which may in turn have a positive effect on the women's adjustment.

The use of a large sample, when carefully described, has the potential for the findings to be generalized to other groups of women, thereby making the findings useful to other practitioners and researchers. It also permits the exploration of the influence of various factors on the outcomes of interest. For example, the above sample consisted of women whose children had a variety of sexual abuse experiences, including intrafamilial and extrafamilial. The large sample size allowed for differences based on these various characteristics to be explored, with the results indicating that characteristics of the abuse experienced by the children were not related to the outcome measures (Hiebert-Murphy 1998, 2000a). Age of the child was, however, related to one outcome variable of interest, namely parenting efficacy. Specifically, the older the child, the lower the mother's sense of competence as a parent. Identifying factors that impact on outcome has obvious implications for intervention. Quantitative research allows for the influence of such factors to be identified and, when appropriate, to be controlled for in subsequent analyses. For example, in the case of parenting efficacy, it was interesting to note that conduct behaviour problems and sexual behaviour problems predicted parenting efficacy even after controlling for the age of the child.

While quantitative research provides much useful information about the role of coping in mediating between the sexual abuse disclosure and outcome measures of interest, it is not without limitations. While the use of standardized assessment measures is an advantage, it places constraints on the data. In responding to such measures, women must fit their coping experiences into predetermined responses that may or may not fully capture women's experiences. There may be ways in which women cope with the disclosure that are not assessed. Furthermore, information on the ways in which a particular woman uses the strategies, under what conditions, in what combinations, etc., is not gathered by this approach. While the design allows for certain variables in the population to be controlled, the uniqueness of particular women in the sample is lost. Hypotheses can be confirmed, but new ideas about the ways in which women cope are not generated. The richness of women's experiences is not fully assessed. Finally, standardized measures examine coping responses in isolation; the context in which certain coping responses are made is not considered, thus limiting our understanding of the complexities of the coping process.

In response to these limitations, current research by the authors has taken a different approach to exploring coping among mothers. This study (Hiebert-Murphy & Burnside 2000) was based on in-depth interviews with women who were dealing with the sexual abuse disclosure of a child. Among other issues, the women were asked about their efforts to cope, factors affecting their coping and the impact of the disclosure.

Women in the study reported using a wide range of behaviours to cope with the disclosure of sexual abuse, including talking to friends, engaging in physical activity, focusing on or taking a leave from paid employment, relying on faith and spirituality, using social services, discharging emotions by crying and advocating for services. Some women acknowledged the use of maladaptive coping strategies such as social withdrawal, avoidance of the sexual abuse topic and drug use. Second, many of the women emphasized the importance of support. Support from members of the women's social network was cited as important in coping; the absence of support was considered to be an additional stressor. The women also talked about the important role that formal supports (e.g., counselling, group therapy) played in their coping. Third, the impact of the responses of social institutions (e.g., the child welfare system, the legal system) to the sexual abuse disclosure was noted. While in some cases the responses of the systems were positive, in other cases the women perceived that the involvement of these systems was not helpful and in fact made coping more challenging. Finally, in discussing their situations, it became apparent that many of the women experienced life circumstances beyond the sexual abuse that taxed their coping resources. For example, the women talked about the financial constraints under which they lived, the abuse that they experienced by their partners, memories of previous abuse in their lives which were triggered by the disclosure, pressures associated with parenting and conflict in their families. These stressors clearly affected the women's abilities to deal with the sexual abuse disclosures.

The use of qualitative methods furthered our understanding of coping in several ways. First of all, it provided an elaboration of the specific strategies that mothers use to cope and led to a greater understanding of the diverse ways in which women attempt to deal with the impact of a sexual abuse disclosure. Second, the findings suggest that coping must be understood as a dynamic process in which individual responses are affected by both intrapersonal and environmental factors. Women's accounts of their experiences strongly suggest that, in order to be understood, the context in which their responses are made must be examined.

Implications for Practice

By raising a number of important issues, the stress-coping model can provide a helpful framework for practitioners concerned with supporting mothers in the post-disclosure period. First of all, practitioners must question the assumptions that they bring to their work and become more aware of how they assess (or judge) mothers' responses to a disclosure of child sexual abuse. The stress-coping model challenges practitioners to consider the broad context when dealing with a mother's reaction to a disclosure. It is imperative to assess stressors in the environment that may affect her reaction. While some of these factors might be directly related to the sexual abuse (e.g., severity, duration, relationship of the abuser to the victim), a number of other factors related to the sexual abuse disclosure must also be considered (e.g., the responses of the child welfare, criminal justice and medical systems; the reaction of members of the family's social network). It must also be acknowledged that the sexual abuse disclosure occurs within a family system that may concurrently be dealing with numerous other stressors such as isolation, poverty and other forms of family violence. While these factors may not be directly related to the abuse, they are likely to affect the way in which the disclosure is experienced and will place constraints on the responses that can be made to the disclosure. Consideration of these factors is likely to cast mothers' behaviours in a different light and offer alternatives to mother blaming.

The stress-coping model further challenges a mother-blaming approach by encouraging practitioners to think about factors that make women resilient. The assumption of this model is that, given sufficient coping resources (which may be internal to the woman or present in the external environment), women will be able to manage the stress in the situation. The fact that some women are able to manage within stressful environments speaks to their strengths and to the resources available to them. The focus is not only on what leads to negative consequences but what facilitates positive outcomes. Practitioners are in a position to actively facilitate coping in a number of ways. On a case-by-case basis they can help mothers by providing emotional support, by educating them about child sexual abuse, by providing opportunities for them to develop the skills they need to deal with the disclosure, by helping them deal with personal issues that are triggered by the disclosure and by linking them with resources that might assist them in coping.

There is also a role for advocacy in promoting coping. Practitioners can empower women by helping them learn about the social service, criminal justice and medical systems and the role these systems play in intervention, by supporting mothers in their efforts to acquire the services that they and their children need and by assisting mothers in developing the skills they need to advocate on their own behalf. In addition, it is important for practitioners to examine the formal supports available to assist women in their coping efforts. Access to treatment programs, shelters (in the case of intrafamilial sexual abuse), financial assistance and employment directly influence the type of responses made by an individual woman. Practitioners need to assess the availability of such supports in order to understand the choices that women make; they must direct their efforts at developing such social supports in order to widen the options for mothers. Practitioners are in a position to lobby for the development of services and programs aimed at supporting women and their children. Such services could include, for example, crisis intervention for families, treatment programs for children and non-offending parents and prevention programs.

The stress-coping framework also points to the role of social policy in understanding mothers. While coping is most often focused on the actions of the individual in a situation, it can also incorporate social factors that create the context in which the individual responses occur. When considering interventions for mothers in families affected by sexual abuse, attention must be given to the practices of social institutions such as child welfare agencies, the police and the medical profession and the extent to which they promote coping and/or are sources of additional stress. How do these systems respond to a disclosure? How are mothers treated by these systems and what role do they have in decisions about intervention? Mother blaming in any of these systems must be identified and challenged. Changes to existing practices and policies may be needed so that mothers are respected, are given power in decision making about their children and families and are provided with supports that strengthen their ability to deal with the abuse.

Finally, a consideration of the effects of social context on coping highlights the need for social change. Social values that hold women solely responsible for what happens to their children and blame them for abuse must be challenged. Barriers that women in general experience in obtaining social equality affect mothers of children who are sexually abused, compromising their ability to cope. Thus, promoting positive change for mothers of children who have been sexually abused cannot be separated from changes required to address other issues affecting women such as poverty, employment equity, availability of child care and violence against women.

Implications for Research

Our research suggests that a stress-coping framework is a useful conceptual model for research. It provides one way of integrating existing research on individual, family and societal factors. For example, the concepts of stressors and coping can account for the findings of previous research on the impact of abuse variables, personality characteristics, history of abuse, social support and social institutions on outcomes such as emotional distress and supportiveness.

The stress-coping model also has the potential for directing future research. The model suggests that it is important for researchers to identify stressors in the situation that challenge the coping resources of mothers and explore the ways in which these stressors affect outcome following a sexual abuse disclosure. Thus far, only a few of these factors have been examined in research (e.g., a history of child sexual abuse, partner violence, the response of the various social institutions to the disclosure). Much work needs to be done to more fully understand the ways in which these particular factors act as stressors. For example, under what conditions do previous sexual abuse experiences impede a mother's ability to deal with her child's sexual abuse disclosure? Are there factors related to the mother's sexual abuse experience that are important in making these experiences risk factors? Are there factors related to the mother's sexual abuse that moderate the extent to which this is a stressor (e.g., having disclosed the abuse, having been believed and supported when the abuse occurred, having received treatment)? In addition, many potential stressors have yet to be examined. These include a range of psychosocial factors at various levels: individual (e.g., problem-solving ability), family (e.g., conflict in the marital relationship) and community (e.g., poverty, availability of programs to support families).

The stress-coping model also suggests that researchers consider factors which have a positive moderating and/or mediating effect on the relationship between the sexual abuse disclosure and adjustment. This includes a consideration of factors that facilitate resilience among women. While the role of social support has been examined, there are many unanswered questions about the influence of various factors such as individual strengths (e.g., assertiveness, self-esteem) and environmental factors (e.g., access to treatment programs for non-offending mothers).

The process of individual coping also requires more attention from researchers. This requires a research strategy that carefully details how each mother copes with the child sexual abuse over time. Research that is longitudinal, is focused on day-to-day and in-depth observations of coping processes and is compatible with a holistic outlook has been identified as badly needed in the area of stress and coping generally (Lazarus 2000); such research would enhance our knowledge of the coping of mothers of children who have been sexually abused and could shed considerable light on many issues, such as our understanding of the interaction between individual coping strategies and environmental supports, the role of formal intervention in enhancing an individual woman's coping ability and the ways in which different types of coping strategies work together in the overall coping process.

Finally, the stress-coping model challenges researchers to study positive outcome, an approach that has generally been underrepresented in coping research (Folkman & Moskowitz 2000). Emotional distress as a measure of adjustment has received the most research attention but is only one dimension to consider in evaluating successful coping. Parenting variables, including the ability to provide support to the child who has been victimized and the ability to perform a range of parenting functions (including instrumental and affective tasks), are examples of other outcomes that could be considered. Given the importance of the response of mothers to their children following disclosure on the outcome for the child (Conte & Berliner 1988; Esparza 1993, Everson et al. 1989), exploring factors that are relevant to understanding various aspects of parenting among these women appears to be an important direction for continued research. Overall, this model allows for a multidimensional conceptualization of outcome and encourages a broad consideration of outcome measures, all of which would enhance our understanding of mothers' experiences.

Conclusion

Integral to intervention in child sexual abuse cases is an appreciation of the experiences of mothers of children who have been sexually abused. Effective intervention in such cases depends on an understanding of how these women are affected by a sexual abuse disclosure and an identification of the factors important in helping them manage the multiple demands they subsequently face. While much attention has been given to clinical opinion about the role of mothers, practice must be based on research that critically examines these assumptions and systematically attempts to understand the reactions and responses of these women. Furthermore, both practice and research would benefit from an integration of research findings and greater efforts to link theory, research and practice. The stress-coping framework is one example of the way in which such integration may occur. This model not only provides a framework to integrate research findings but suggests important directions for future research (using both qualitative and quantitative .nethodologies). It provides practitioners with a conceptualization of mothers that encourages an assessment of both environmental and individual factors, and supports interventions that are broad-based. Such an approach to practice is likely the most appropriate to address the complexities of child sexual abuse.

Chapter 3

Treatment for Children Who Have Experienced Sexual Abuse

Rayleen V. De Luca and Alana D. Grayston

Introduction

Since the early 1980s, child sexual abuse has captured the sustained attention of mental health professionals, as well as the public at large. Its exact prevalence is unknown, but recent Canadian studies suggest that approximately 16 percent of males and 32 percent of females may experience one or more unwanted sexual contacts prior to the age of seventeen (e.g., Bagley 1991a; Bagley, Wood & Young 1994). As some victims may be unable to recall early experiences of sexual abuse (Williams 1994) or may be reluctant to disclose them as adults (Barnett, Miller-Perrin & Perrin 1997), these figures are likely to underestimate the true extent of the problem.

Although "it is clear that no single symptom or pattern of symptoms is present in all victims" and that "some ... victims exhibit no symptoms at all" (Barnett et al. 1997: 87), a growing body of research suggests that children may be vulnerable to a number of difficulties following experiences of victimization (e.g., Beitchman et al. 1991; Kendall-Tackett, Williams & Finkelhor 1993; Wolfe & Birt 1995), including internalizing and externalizing behaviour problems (e.g., anxiety, aggression; Einbender & Friedrich 1989; Friedrich, Urquiza & Beilke 1986; Inderbitzen-Pisaruk, Shawchuck & Hoier 1992) and disrupted sexual development or premature sexualization (e.g., preoccupation with sexual matters, compulsive masturbation, sexual acting out; Einbender & Friedrich 1989; Friedrich et al. 1986; Inderbitzen-Pisaruk et al. 1992). Other documented sequelae of sexual abuse in children include low self-esteem, depression and academic and social problems (e.g., Einbender & Friedrich 1989; Grayston, De Luca & Boyes 1992; Inderbitzen-Pisaruk et al. 1992; Tong, Oates & McDowell 1987). Child sexual abuse is also implicated in the occurrence of many severe and chronic problems during adolescence and later life, such as suicidal behaviour, revictimization, prostitution, sexual offending and drug and alcohol abuse (e.g., Bagley et al. 1994; Boney-McCoy & Finkelhor 1995; Briere & Runtz 1986; Grayston & De Luca 1999; Nadon 1990; Romano & De Luca 1996; Saunders et al. 1999).

Growing awareness of these serious sequelae has dramatized the need to develop effective and timely interventions for children who have been sexually abused. Over the past decade, therapy services for victimized children have received considerable attention (e.g., De Luca et al. 1992; De Luca, Grayston & Romano 1999; Finkelhor & Berliner 1995; Friedrich 1990; Gil 1996; Reeker, Ensing & Elliott 1997). Practitioners have utilized a variety of methods, including individual and group psychotherapy for boys and girls (e.g., De Luca et al. 1992; De Luca et al. 1999; Gil 1991) and family-based interventions (e.g., Gil 1996) to address the negative effects of victimization and to serve the ever-increasing number of children referred for treatment of abuse.

Assessment

Assessment is an integral component of any treatment intervention and must be an ongoing process throughout therapy. While a thorough discussion of procedures for evaluating sexually abused children and their families is not possible within the context of this chapter, several points would seem crucial to mention. First, in order to select appropriate treatment strategies for children who have been sexually abused, it is essential that clinicians initially conduct a comprehensive evaluation of the child's psychological, educational and social functioning (James 1989). Careful examination of contextual factors that may influence the impact of the abuse, such as the degree of family support (Wolfe & Gentile 1992), or impair the family's ability to adequately function, such as chronic stressors (Gil 1996), is also of critical importance and may highlight additional areas to target as part of the intervention. Once a child's strengths and resources have been identified, along with his or her symptoms and concerns, the clinician can develop a treatment plan aimed at reducing the negative effects of the sexual abuse, assisting the child in mastering appropriate developmental tasks and preventing further victimization (Walker & Bolkovatz 1988). A review of specific procedures for evaluating abused children and their families may be found in several excellent sources, including Friedrich (1990), Waterman and Lusk (1993), Wolfe and Gentile (1992) and Shapiro (1991).

Treatment

Although the specific impact of sexual abuse varies from case to case and may be influenced by a number of factors, such as characteristics of the abuse, qualities of the familial and social environment and characteristics of the victimized child (e.g., frequency and duration of sexual contact, reactions of significant others at the time of discovery / disclosure, gender—see Barnett et al. 1997; Becker & Bonner 1998; Berliner & Elliott 1996), there is a general consensus in the literature that psychotherapy is "an important part of the healing process" (Tingus et al. 1996: 63) and that some form of therapy is indicated for most victims of sexual abuse (Friedrich 1990). Many children, however, do not receive therapy services following victimization (Tingus et al. 1996). Preliminary studies, for example, suggest that treatment entry may be contingent on a variety of factors, such as the age and ethnicity of the child, the frequency and severity of the abuse and the involvement of law enforcement and child protection officials (Tingus et al. 1996).

When treatment is offered to sexually abused children, individual therapy appears to be the most common form of intervention, although group- and family-based therapies are also frequently employed (Keller, Cicchinelli & Gardner 1989). A multimodal approach, tailored to the child's level of developmental and cognitive functioning, may hold particular promise as a means of redressing the negative effects of sexual abuse (Bonner et al. 1992), with different interventions (e.g., individual, group and family therapy) being utilized at different stages of the therapeutic process to comprehensively address the needs of the child and her or his family. Regardless of the modality selected, "work with children inevitably includes work with adults, and a family focus often is essential" (Webb 1991: 39). As we have noted elsewhere (De Luca et al. 1999), close collaboration with children's caregivers is a critical element of any treatment program, not only to empower and support the important adults in a child's life, but also to increase the probability that therapeutic gains will generalize to the real day-to-day world.

Individual Therapy

While numerous approaches have been utilized in individual treatment with children who have been sexually abused, play therapy and cognitive behavioural therapy are among the interventions most frequently described in the clinical and empirical literature.

Play Therapy

"Play is considered the child's natural medium for rehearsing new developmental skills" and "working through conflicts" (Walker & Bolkovatz 1988: 249), and as such, may be a particularly appropriate form of treatment for children under ten or eleven years of age (Walker & Bolkovatz 1988; Webb 1991). The utilization of play materials allows children to express feelings and deal with painful issues symbolically, at a comfortable distance, and at a safe, self-directed pace, without the need for verbal discourse. At the same time, it serves as a means of establishing a close relationship with a supportive and caring adult, which may help the abused child regain a sense of interpersonal trust (Walker & Bolkovatz 1988; Webb 1991). According to Walker and Bolkovatz (1988: 268), play therapy also helps to "prevent developmental delays that cause secondary trauma ... and ... [it] teaches the child how to positively control his or her world again."

Play therapy with abused children is based on developmental principles and is designed to help young children work through the traumatic events to which they have been exposed. Through the use of play materials, such as dolls, puppets, arts and crafts supplies, board games and other objects, children can begin to address the multiplicity of issues surrounding their abuse (Webb 1991), including the fear and anxiety that are often associated with disclosure (Berliner & Wheeler 1987). The treatment process is facilitated by the therapist's efforts to support and encourage the child in discussing various aspects of the abuse (Webb 1991). As several authors have noted, "free play or undirected arts activities, in and of themselves, will not bring about insight, growth, or rehabilitation for the victim of sexual abuse" (Naitove 1982: 283); it is "the therapist's interventions and utilizations of the play [that] are critical" (Chethik 1989: 49).

To date, a number of approaches to play therapy have been described in the clinical literature (for reviews, see O'Connor & Schaefer 1994; Schaefer & O'Connor 1983). Depending upon the treatment philosophy of the therapist, either a non-directive or structured approach may be utilized with abuse victims, although the literature would suggest that it is important to employ a variety of play materials and techniques in working with this child client group (Webb 1991).

While the healing power of play therapy has been documented (Gil 1991; Marvasti 1994), most of the data regarding its effectiveness are anecdotal and come from single case reports. Strand (1991), for example, recently described a play therapy program for a six-year-old girl who had experienced sexual abuse, indicating that the child was able to successfully deal with the trauma of her experience through the use of structured and unstructured play in a safe and nurturing environment. Preliminary studies using standardized outcome measures (e.g., De Luca et al. 1993; Friedrich & Reams 1987) also suggest that play therapy may be an effective intervention for abused and non-abused children, although much more research is required to empirically document the potential value of this treatment approach, as some outcome studies have failed to find significant differences in the functioning of mal-treated children following time-limited play treatment (e.g., Reams & Friedrich 1994). For a comprehensive description of play therapy strat-egies for use with sexually abused children, the interested reader may wish to consult Walker and Bolkovatz (1988), Webb (1991), Gil (1991) and Marvasti (1994).

Cognitive Behavioural Therapy

Given that some victimized children appear to exhibit symptoms con-sistent with post-traumatic stress disorder or PTSD, such as high levels of anxiety and repetitive and intrusive thoughts regarding the abuse (McLeer et al. 1988), many clinicians have begun to utilize cognitive behavioural treatment procedures in their interventions with abuse victims (for a comprehensive description, see Deblinger & Heflin 1996). These techniques are designed to assist children in gradually confront-ing thoughts, feelings and memories regarding their abuse (Deblinger, Steer & Lippmann 1999), in order to extinguish the traumatic response. It is essential for treatment to re-expose the abused child to traumatic cues in a safe and structured setting:

> The desire to protect children from further discomfort by shield-ing them from trauma-related cues is well-intentioned, [al-though] … it is not always in the children's best interest. In working with traumatized children, a willingness to discuss the traumatic situation openly and to assist the child in dealing with *all* disturbing aspects of the event without shying away from any of the traumatic cues is critical, not only to produce positive treatment gains, but also to avoid the potential iatro-genic effects of signaling to the child that the traumatic memo-ries are too horrible to face and master. (Lyons 1987: 354)

Recent empirical studies suggest that this approach to treatment may hold significant promise as a means of reducing the negative effects of sexual abuse in children and adolescents.

Deblinger, McLeer and Henry (1990), for example, utilized a vari-ety of cognitive behavioural techniques, including gradual exposure to abuse-related memories, training in coping skills, such as relaxation and anger management, and education regarding sexual abuse and personal safety training in their work with nineteen girls, aged three to sixteen, who had experienced sexual abuse. Children were seen indi-vidually over a period of twelve weeks, while non-offending caregivers participated in a separate intervention designed to provide them with (a) information regarding the consequences of sexual abuse, (b) train-ing in behaviour management and (c) instruction regarding parent-child communication and modelling of adaptive coping behaviour. Objective and standardized assessments were completed before, during and after the therapeutic intervention, with findings at post-treatment suggesting significant reductions in children's symptoms of general anxiety, PTSD and depression. Similar gains were reported in a subsequent study examining the efficacy of parent-only, child-only and parent-child cognitive behavioural therapy conditions (Deblinger, Lippmann & Steer 1996).

A more recent study conducted by Farrell, Hains and Davies (1998) utilized a cognitive behavioural intervention with four sexually abused children between the ages of eight and ten. Treatment emphasized training in relaxation skills, positive self-talk and cognitive restructuring. Outcomes were assessed at post-treatment and at a three-month follow-up using standardized measures of PTSD, anxiety and depression. Results suggested that the therapy program was effective, with all participants experiencing decreases in PTSD symptomatology over the course of the intervention.

Recent studies also indicate that cognitive behavioural therapy may be a useful approach relative to non-directive or supportive forms of treatment. In research conducted with preschoolers and their parents, for example, Cohen and Mannarino (1996b) compared the effectiveness of a twelve-week individual cognitive behavioural program with a less structured intervention. The cognitive behavioural program specifically targeted many of the symptoms commonly observed in children who have experienced sexual abuse, including sexually inappropriate behaviours, aggression, sadness and regressive behaviours (for a detailed description of the treatment model, see Cohen & Mannarino 1993). Results indicated that individuals receiving the abuse-focused, cognitive behavioural intervention showed significant improvements on most outcome measures over the course of treatment, while those receiving non-directive, supportive treatment experienced no significant changes in symptomatology. Positive findings were also obtained in a subsequent study with older children, aged seven to fourteen years, in which abuse-specific cognitive behavioural treatment was again compared with a non-directive therapeutic approach (Cohen & Mannarino 1998b).

While these initial results are highly encouraging, further research is required to evaluate the long-term stability of changes resulting from cognitive behavioural interventions. Such studies are now beginning to appear in the literature on therapy outcome, and suggest that sexually abused children may sustain therapy gains for up to one or two years following treatment (Cohen & Mannarino 1997; Deblinger et al. 1999).

Group Therapy

Group therapy is another common intervention in cases of sexual abuse (Sturkie 1992) and is widely regarded as a valuable component of the treatment process for abuse victims (Haugaard & Reppucci 1988), if not "the treatment of choice" (Steward et al. 1986: 263). Over the past two decades, a large number of articles have appeared in the clinical literature touting the potential benefits of group treatment and offering detailed descriptions of therapy groups for children who have been sexually abused (e.g., Berliner & Ernst 1984; Berman 1990; De Luca et al. 1992; De Luca et al. 1999; Friedrich et al. 1988; Kitchur & Bell 1989; Kweller & Ray 1992). To date, group interventions have emphasized a variety of treatment goals, such as (a) clarifying abuse dynamics; (b) helping children to identify, label and express feelings; (c) enhancing self-esteem and personal safety; (d) reducing symptomatic behaviour and (e) helping children to develop a variety of communication, social and problem-solving skills (e.g., De Luca et al. 1992; De Luca et al. 1999).

Although there are, as yet, few empirical studies comparing the relative utility of individual, group and family therapies in the treatment of sexual abuse, numerous clinicians have suggested that a group experience may offer abused children several advantages over other interventions:

(1) By allowing boys and girls to interact with peers who have disclosed similar traumatic events, groups may serve to reduce the sense of isolation and stigmatization reported by many abuse victims (Berliner & Ernst 1984) and may help to nurture the formation of supportive relationships with other children (Peake 1987). In these respects, the group experience may be particularly effective in redressing some of the negative effects of sexual abuse, such as low self-esteem and difficulties with interpersonal trust, and in promoting mastery of age-appropriate developmental tasks, such as cultivation of same-sex friendships.

(2) By allowing therapists to provide services to several children at one time, groups may be more cost-effective than other interventions, such as individual treatment (Haugaard & Reppucci 1988). In the context of limited therapy resources and a growing demand for service, the use of group treatment may be an effective means of increasing children's access to timely intervention following sexual abuse.

(3) By countering some of the potentially threatening aspects of individual treatment, such as the formation of a confidential and intense relationship with a single powerful adult (Sturkie 1992), and of family-based interventions, such as regular contact with the offender, group therapy may also help to minimize any anxiety children feel about seeking clinical services. This may be an important factor to

consider in the treatment-planning process, given that therapy participation may be influenced, at least in part, by the perceived acceptability of an intervention (Wolf 1978).

Although several preliminary studies have begun to empirically document the effectiveness of group interventions (e.g., Friedrich et al. 1992; Hall-Marley & Damon 1993; Kitchur & Bell 1989; Kruczek & Vitanza 1999), at this time, there remains an overall paucity of treatment outcome research in the area of sexual abuse (Finkelhor & Berliner 1995; Reeker et al. 1997). In an effort to help redress this gap in the literature on group treatment, our research team recently initiated a series of studies to examine the utility of a group therapy program for boys and girls who had been sexually abused.

University of Manitoba Research Program on Group Therapy
Over the past decade, a number of sexually abused children have participated in therapy groups at the University of Manitoba (e.g., De Luca et al. 1995; De Luca, Hazen & Cutler 1993; Grayston & De Luca 1995, 1996; Hack, Osachuk & De Luca 1994; Hiebert-Murphy, De Luca & Runtz 1992; Romano et al. 1996). Children have been referred to the groups by parents, organizations within the community, such as schools, other treatment providers, such as individual therapists, and child protection officials. Children have been considered for inclusion in our program if they meet several criteria:

(1) The child has previously made a disclosure of intrafamilial and/or third-party sexual abuse.
(2) The child is currently living in a safe environment, away from the alleged perpetrator(s). ·
(3) The child has no characteristics (e.g., acute suicidal ideation, severe behavioural problems) which would make group treatment an inappropriate intervention.
(4) The child and his/her family are interested in receiving group therapy services.
(5) The child has access to supervised transportation to and from weekly group meetings.

While some clinicians (e.g., Berliner & Ernst 1984) have discussed the potential utility of treating male and female victims within a single group, we have opted to provide separate programs for girls and boys, as the literature suggests that there may be sex differences in children's treatment needs and reactions to sexual abuse (e.g., Berliner & Elliott 1996; Rogers & Terry 1984). In our experience, it has not been necessary to form separate groups for victims of intrafamilial, as opposed to third-party abuse, although we have certainly made every effort to keep our groups as homogeneous as possible, in order to guard against the possibility that any child will feel different from her or his peers (De Luca et al. 1999).

Group referrals have been evaluated prior to and following treatment, with a range of assessment measures, including the Child Behavior Checklist (Achenbach 1991), the Child Sexual Behavior Inventory (Friedrich et al. 1991), the Revised Children's Manifest Anxiety Scale (Reynolds & Richmond 1978) and the Self-Esteem Inventory (Coopersmith 1981). Referral forms and background questionnaires have also been completed by referral sources and caregivers prior to group commencement, to provide therapists with information regarding the child's family, current functioning and history of sexual abuse. Data obtained from these assessments have been used to screen potential group candidates, evaluate some of the effects of sexual abuse on the children and identify general areas that may be important to target in group therapy sessions. In addition, assessment findings have been used as a means of gauging the effectiveness of the group treatment program.

Following an initial screening session, children have participated in single-gender therapy groups of nine to twelve weeks duration. Groups have generally consisted of six to eight children, whose ages fall within a relatively limited span, such as seven to nine years or eight to eleven years. Therapists have typically been graduate students enrolled in the clinical psychology and social work programs at the University of Manitoba. Based on the recommendation of Adams-Tucker and Adams (1984), therapists have, for the most part, been of the same gender as group members, with two female therapists generally facilitating the girls' program and two male therapists providing the intervention to boys. When these combinations have been unavailable, however, we have successfully offered boys' groups using two female therapists or a male-female therapy team.

For all groups, sessions have lasted ninety minutes and have followed a standard four-part format (see De Luca et al. 1992; De Luca et al. 1999). Each session, for example, has begun with fifteen minutes of *circle time*, during which therapists and children review the events of the previous week and discuss the agenda for the current session. During *activity time*, forty-five minutes have been devoted to specific tasks (e.g., discussion, crafts, puppet shows, movies) that focus on abuse-related issues and themes, such as feelings about the offender, self-esteem, sex education and prevention of sexual abuse. Detailed descriptions of the materials and methods utilized in *activity time* have been presented elsewhere (e.g., De Luca et al. 1992; De Luca et al. 1999). Group activities have been followed each week by twenty minutes of *diary time*, which allows children to write or draw about group themes in private scrapbooks supplied by the therapists. The last ten minutes of each session have been reserved for *snack time,* during which therapists summarize the session's themes and praise the children for their efforts.

One of the most challenging aspects of providing group services to sexually abused children is finding effective ways to manage the many inappropriate behaviours, such as name-calling and refusing to listen, which may appear as children begin to address particularly difficult issues in the group (e.g., feelings about the offender). To date, we have relied on several strategies to minimize these behaviours, including creation of group rules and implementation of a group reward program to encourage appropriate conduct in sessions (e.g., De Luca et al. 1999; Hack et al. 1994).

While empirical literature demonstrating the effectiveness of group treatment is relatively scarce (Reeker et al. 1997), some of our initial findings at the University of Manitoba have been quite encouraging. De Luca et al. (1993), for example, assessed the effectiveness of a ten-week group intervention with seven girls, aged ten to eleven, who had experienced intrafamilial abuse. Issues addressed during the ninety-minute sessions included feelings about the offender, family changes following disclosure, responsibility for the abuse, body image, self-esteem, sex education and personal safety. Standardized measures completed by parents and children during pre- and post-treatment assessments indicated significant improvements in several areas over the course of the intervention, with girls reporting higher self-esteem and lower anxiety, and caregivers acknowledging fewer internalizing and externalizing behaviour problems, such as depression or aggressive behaviour, following group treatment. Parent-reported problem behaviours also declined during a nine-week group intervention with five seven- to nine-year-old girls, although self-report measures appeared less useful in evaluating therapeutic gains among these younger children (Hiebert-Murphy et al. 1992).

More recently, De Luca et al. (1995) examined the effectiveness of group treatment for thirty-five girls, aged seven to twelve, who had experienced sexual abuse. Each of the girls participated in a semistructured therapy group of nine to twelve weeks duration. Issues explored during the sessions included feelings about the offender, sex education, problem solving and prevention of further abuse. Measures of self-esteem, anxiety and behaviour problems were administered to parents and children prior to and following treatment at one- and nine-to twelve-month intervals. Thirty-five girls with no known history of sexual abuse provided comparison group data for anxiety and self-esteem. Findings indicated that self-esteem increased, and anxiety and behaviour problems decreased over the course of group treatment, with most gains being maintained at the nine- to twelve-month follow-up. Comparison group data provided further support for the utility of group treatment as a means of enhancing the self-esteem of abuse victims. Social validity reports of children and caregivers also confirmed the potential value of group treatment, with most participants and parents acknowledging that the group experience had been helpful and worthwhile.

In general, similar data have been obtained in our evaluations of boys' therapy groups. Hack et al. (1994), for example, utilizing standardized measures, found that boys tended to experience increases in self-esteem and decreases in depression following a twelve-week group intervention, as well as reductions in parent-reported internalizing and externalizing behaviour problems. Boys receiving group therapy also experienced some improvements in adjustment and behaviour in a recent study by Grayston and De Luca (1995), with parent reports of internalizing, externalizing and sexual behaviour problems tending to decline from the pre- to post-treatment assessments. While the differences between treated and untreated children did not reach statistical significance in this latter study, improvements on all measures tended to be larger for boys involved in the therapy group. At the same time, however, examination of therapy gains on a case-by-case basis revealed considerable variability in the effects of the intervention, with some children experiencing clinically significant changes during treatment and other boys experiencing less extensive or limited improvement. Of particular interest, given this variability, was the finding that caregivers and children almost uniformly described the group experience as positive, helpful and worthwhile (Grayston & De Luca 1996).

Taken as a whole, our research results suggest that further evaluation of the group model is warranted at this time. While short-term groups appear to promote positive changes in adjustment and behaviour for male and female victims of abuse, they are clearly not a panacea, and many children may require additional therapy to address abuse-related issues and themes. Longer group programs, in combination with additional services for family members, will likely be required in many cases to fully address pertinent issues and maximize treatment gains. More widespread application of a "parallel group model" (Hall-Marley & Damon 1993), for example, in which abused children and non-offending caregivers concurrently attend similar therapy groups, may be a particularly promising direction for future clinical and empirical work.

Family Therapy

Given that parents and siblings appear vulnerable to psychological distress following a child's disclosure (e.g., DiPietro 1987; Hiebert-

Murphy 1998), and that family functioning is often associated with children's recovery from sexual abuse and risk for further maltreatment (Berliner & Elliott 1996), many clinicians contend that family therapy is an essential component of treatment in most cases of sexual abuse (e.g., Sgroi 1982a). While little information is currently available regarding the impact of family-based treatment (Barnett et al. 1997; Berliner & Elliott 1996), reviews of outcome research have been cautiously optimistic about the effectiveness of family therapy as a treatment modality for children who have been sexually abused (Johnson, Rasbury & Siegel 1986).

Adams-Tucker and Adams (1984: 67) have cautioned against the use of "family group therapy" with children whose abuse was perpetrated by a family member. Instead of including the offender in treatment sessions, they recommend that only those persons in the family who may aid the child in healing be included in the therapy. In a similar vein, Porter, Blick and Sgroi (1982: 144) have emphasized that, in cases of incest, family therapy should not be utilized unless the parents are willing to take responsibility for the sexual abuse of the child: "The perpetrator must admit responsibility for the abuse, apologize to the child, and reassure the child that it will not happen again. The nonoffending parent must take responsibility for not protecting the child." According to Porter et al. (1982: 144), during treatment,

> the family [also] needs to discuss as a whole, the emotional pain associated with the sexual abuse, the role reversal which took place, the need for children to be permitted to engage in age-appropriate behaviour, the blurred boundaries, the poor communication patterns, the need to learn good parenting skills, and the need for expansion of social and support systems for all members.

They recommend that family therapy always be used in conjunction with other treatment modalities.

Although family therapists generally agree that the goal of treatment is the effective functioning of the family system, there are widely discrepant opinions as to how this goal is best achieved. Family therapy includes a number of approaches, including psychodynamic (Ackerman 1966), communications (Jackson 1957), structural (Minuchin 1974) and behavioural (Liberman 1972). Specific applications of family therapy in cases of sexual abuse may be found in a number of sources, including Friedrich (1990) and Gil (1996).

Conclusions

While a growing body of empirical research is beginning to document the effectiveness of individual, group and family therapies in cases of sexual abuse, further evaluation of treatment outcomes for victimized children is nevertheless required. Additional studies, identifying the specific factors associated with treatment success in cases of sexual abuse (e.g., Cohen & Mannarino 1996a, 1998a; Grayston et al. 1997; Merrick, Allen & Crase 1994) and involving larger samples of children, long-term follow-up assessments and more assessment and outcome measures, will likely prove instrumental in accurately gauging the utility of current interventions and in determining which children will and will not benefit from various treatment modalities. In particular, more widespread utilization of abuse-specific outcome measures that directly tap the behavioural and emotional sequelae most commonly linked with sexual abuse (e.g., sexualized behaviours) as well as the traumagenic dynamics that appear to be inherent in the experience of victimization (e.g., feelings of powerlessness and betrayal; see Finkelhor & Browne 1985), may greatly assist clinicians and researchers in their attempts to fully evaluate the impact of existing treatment procedures. Further examination of therapy gains on a case-by-case basis may also yield valuable information regarding the effectiveness of various modalities, by permitting researchers and practitioners to make specific inferences about the direction, magnitude and meaning of change for a particular family or child. To date, most evaluation studies have focused on typical or group-based outcomes, significantly limiting our ability to comment on the utility of various interventions for individual victims of sexual abuse. While it is helpful to know that, on average, program participants may experience improvements following treatment, more detailed information regarding the nature and extent of these changes is clearly required if clinicians and researchers are to properly assess the adequacy of available therapies and the need for further intervention. Single-case research designs, similar to those employed by Romano (1999) with adult male survivors of sexual abuse, could be readily adapted to treatment outcome studies involving children and families and would add to the existing empirical literature by providing this essential individualized focus. As researchers progress in their investigation of treatment outcomes using these and other strategies, important data will undoubtedly be forthcoming regarding the relative merits of available therapeutic interventions. Information of this kind is essential to ensure that clinicians are providing abused children with services that are maximally effective.

In the meantime, the clinical and empirical literature would suggest that several factors may be important for practitioners to consider in their work with abuse victims. A growing body of evidence, for example, is beginning to indicate that abuse-focused interventions are more useful in addressing the sequelae of victimization than non-directive or supportive forms of treatment (e.g., Cohen & Mannarino 1996b, 1998b), and that clinicians may, therefore, need to adopt a fairly active role in therapy sessions if they hope to adequately meet the needs of victimized girls and boys. Given the multiplicity of complex issues confronting families in which a child has been sexually abused, as well as the sometimes variable effects of short-term interventions (e.g., Grayston & De Luca 1995), practitioners must also be prepared to offer abused children and their families a range of comprehensive treatment options.

Given that many children do not disclose abusive experiences, and, as a result, are unable to benefit from the treatment services available to identified victims, it is also critical that clinicians and researchers expand their approach to the problem of abuse by developing and evaluating programs to prevent its occurrence. Over the past two decades, numerous home- and school-based interventions have been created for children in an effort to teach them concepts and skills that may reduce their vulnerability to victimization (e.g., how to distinguish appropriate and inappropriate touch) and to encourage disclosure. While a growing body of research suggests that these programs may be effective in improving children's knowledge regarding personal safety and sexual abuse (e.g., MacMillan et al. 1994; Rispens, Aleman & Goudena 1997; Tutty 1993; Wurtele 1998), to date, very little is known about "the real-world effectiveness of [such] instruction" (Finkelhor, Asdigian & Dziuba-Leatherman 1995: 142). Further research, examining children's responses to actual threats and assaults, will likely prove instrumental in improving the quality of existing programs.

Ultimately, however, the prevention of sexual abuse must be addressed in a more comprehensive and coordinated fashion if significant progress is to be made in reducing the incidence of victimization. Community efforts must be broadened to address the full range of individual and societal factors that may potentially contribute to the occurrence of sexual abuse (such factors as child pornography, weak criminal sanctions against perpetrators and inadequate supervision of children are identified by Finkelhor 1984), rather than focusing disproportionate attention on training potential victims to avoid or resist abuse. Efforts of this kind, in combination with improvements to existing prevention and treatment programs for children, may hold considerable promise as a means of reducing the incidence and effects of sexual abuse.

Chapter 4

Incest Does Not Just Happen
Grooming Behaviours and Processes among Paternal Incest Offenders
Christine Kreklewetz

Introduction

The prevalence rates for child sexual abuse in Canada and the United States are alarmingly high. A recent U.S. national study estimated that 15 to 32 percent of children are sexually abused (Vogeltanz et al. 1999). Approximately one in four girls will be sexually abused before age eighteen (Finkelhor, Hotaling, Lewis & Smith 1990; Russell 1986). Children are frequently sexually abused by a relative or immediate family member (Russell 1986; Ward 1984). In many cases the abuser is the father or a father figure (Finkelhor 1984), and the breach of such a trusting relationship carries with it more severe long-term effects for the survivor (Finkelhor 1979; Russell 1986).

Sexual offences themselves do not just happen; rather, they have been described as "a culmination of a long series or chain of events" (Nelson & Jackson 1989: 167). In contrast to popular belief, there often lie many progressive planned steps between the initial urge to offend and the resulting sexual offence. While these planned steps are not causes of incest, they are "grooming behaviours" that allow incest offenders to access their victims, create the opportunity to offend, enhance the victims' compliance and lead up to the offence. This research project with incestuous child molesters identifies specific grooming behaviours in incest and paternal incest offenders' perceptions of the influence of societal factors on their offending behaviours.

Knowledge about the strategies offenders use to get close to their victims and gain their trust is critical for both prevention and recognition of incest. There is little research that examines the larger context of the abusive incident, specifically the pre-offence processes that are affected by the family environment, societal influences and the perpetrator's feelings, thoughts and premeditated behaviours. We know very little about offender grooming behaviours from the perpetrator's perspective and no studies to date have examined the multiple contextual factors leading up to the offences from the offender's viewpoint.

Only a handful of studies have examined the grooming processes of incest offenders. Christiansen and Blake (1990) identified several specific grooming behaviours: (a) building trust by giving gifts to, and spending time with, the victim, (b) favouritism, (c) alienating the victim from friends, (d) boundary violations in personal environments such as hygiene tasks and (e) inappropriate sexual conversations. Young (1997) showed how offenders situate their grooming behaviours within the context of routine activities such as playing games, caretaking activities, domestic chores and family interaction and socialization. According to Young (1997), offenders used normalization to disguise their abuse and legitimate physical contact between the child and themselves. One study with twenty male sex offenders (Conte, Wolf & Smith 1989) revealed how offenders deliberately select child victims who appear more vulnerable. The offenders gained access to the children by desensitizing the children to touch and verbal discussions about sex. Gilgun and Connor (1989) interviewed fourteen male sex offenders and found that setting up the situation to abuse was crucial in the victimization process. This made the offence more pleasurable for the offender. These studies provide critical information on grooming behaviours; however, with the exception of Christiansen and Blake's (1990) research, the above studies did not focus exclusively on paternal incest offenders. They grouped intrafamilial and extrafamilial offenders together and included victims outside the family and victims of both sexes.

In our society, certain social values and beliefs may influence offenders' thinking and behaviour. Male and female socialization influence our attitudes and beliefs about how individuals should function within families. Male gender socialization has been implicated in sexual violence towards women and children (Lisak, Hopper & Song 1996; Russell 1986) and is critical in understanding incest. Finkelhor (1987) locates the problem of sexual abuse within the normal processes of male socialization. He proposes that male socialization teaches men to get their emotional needs met through sexual relationships which involve, in his terms, "sexualization of emotional expression." The "attraction gradient" encourages women to be attracted to older, larger and more powerful men and leads men to look for younger, smaller and less powerful persons than themselves. The fact that society also exempts men from caregiving responsibilities for children results in many men not understanding their role in children's care, nurturing and protection.

Media representations, such as those portrayed on billboards and television and in magazines and movies, carry stimulating messages that sexualize women, youth and children, thus desensitizing society and contributing to violence against women as well as incest. There is also a proliferation of child pornography which views adult-child sexual activity as acceptable. Research suggests that both the societal acceptability of adult-child sexual activity and the exposure to sexually violent materials perpetuate and reinforce sex offender behaviour (Hayashino, Wurtele & Klebe 1995; Malamuth 1981).

Finkelhor (1986a), in an extensive review of theories which explain sexual abuse of children, concluded that no single-factor theory fully explains sexual abuse. Maddock and Larson's (1995) ecological model of incest recognizes the complexity of incestuous behaviour and the larger contextual elements that influence its occurrence. These include individual, structural and functional patterns of family interaction and sociocultural influences on gender identity and behaviour. Maddock and Larson explain incest as arising primarily from distortions in family sexuality. The structure of an incestuous family is dysfunctional: boundaries are distorted, and sexuality is used to exploit its members . According to Maddock and Larson, incest arises from a complex interaction of social context variables: intrapsychic influences (e.g., mental disorders, early life disturbances, low self-esteem); relational variables (e.g., power imbalances between the genders in the family); developmental variables (e.g., ineffective coping strategies for change) and situational factors (e.g., opportunity and disinhibitory substances such as alcohol use). We can thus conceptualize grooming behaviours as deliberately planned actions and processes leading up to the incest in which individual, familial, social and cultural forces play a role.

In order to better understand the interactions of these contextual elements and to further explore offenders' grooming behaviours, a study of paternal incest offenders was undertaken.

Interviews with Fathers

Thirteen audiotaped interviews with offenders took place at a Canadian minimum security federal penitentiary between April and August 1997. The participants were fathers or father figures who were primary caregivers to their female victim(s). The men participated in in-depth interviews which lasted between 1.5 and 2.5 hours.

The men were between twenty-nine and sixty-three years of age. Five men had less than grade twelve education, three had completed grade twelve, two had university or college courses and three had a university or college degree. Their sentences for sexual assault or sexual interference ranged from two to eight years. Time spent in group counselling ranged from three to twenty-one months. Three of the men had more than one victim. Five men had abused their biological daughters, and eight men had abused their step-daughters or their girl-friends' daughters. Eleven men described being emotionally, physically and/or sexually abused by family members or relatives.

A qualitative analysis of these interviews consisted of classifying emerging patterns and characteristics across and within interviews and highlighting relationships that connected statements and events within specific contexts. Also considered significant in the analysis were topics that participants spontaneously mentioned (e.g., derogatory comments about women).

Grooming Behaviours
Awareness of Grooming Behaviours and Patterns
It was difficult for participants in the study to identify and/or acknowledge specific grooming behaviours. Denial and minimization appeared prevalent among offenders even after treatment. One father, who had gone through extensive counselling, said:

> That's probably the hardest thing as an offender to understand—and certainly for me. That's been something that I've struggled with—I can say "Nooo, it just happened" and that's the easiest way of—[laugh]—kind of, rationalizing it. No, there's planning ... it may not be overt and sort of in the front of your mind or say that I'm going to do this and do this and do this, but in the back of your mind set up the situation.

Many of the men maintained that they did not plan their offences. One father, who at the beginning of the interview denied any planning, later spoke of taking advantage of "opportunities" to put the children to bed when his wife was away from home. Another father rationalized not recalling any abuse, let alone his grooming behaviours:

> I think what would happen was as soon as I'd offend, I'd blank them out ... because I knew I couldn't live with this ... she'd say nothing to me and I'd say nothing to her.... I heard one time [my daughter] say something that this was just like the Brady Bunch—everything looks so good on the outside and yet....

Another father's denial of grooming also took the form of presenting his family as a kind of "Brady Bunch": "We probably had the best family in the world. We traveled all over the place, enjoyed each other. Every one of us was ... involved in all kinds of sports activities.... We went to church."

Many of the men minimized their offending by stating that they had a difficult time remembering details of the grooming since in some cases the abuse occurred thirty years earlier. In other cases, the men claimed that heavy alcohol and/or drug use at the time dulled their memory. One man recognized that his use of minimization and denial was so strong that, when confronted about the incest by his adult daughter years later, he stated,

> I couldn't believe that those were things I've done.... The shock to me was so great that I was going to get a lawyer and counishcharge her for defamation, or whatever it was, because I was under denial. I was denying it. It's not until I started taking programs and really looking into myself and dig down there.

One man at first denied planning his offence with the distortion that "the offence happened by accident." Thinking back, he said,

> I would do those things without actually thinking that I am going to, uh, assault her, but I would do them with the idea that, "Well, I'll get her ready just in case I want to." That was more the kind of thinking. So things just didn't happen by accident ... say ninety percent of the time ... uh, when an assault took place there was a lead-up period to it.

Selecting the Victims

Selecting the victim was a critical component of the grooming process and often began with selecting women as partners who had certain characteristics. Some men sought out women whom they could control and manipulate, who lacked independence and assertiveness and who may have had a background of child or spousal abuse themselves. As one man stated, "I would spend hours looking for just that certain woman who ... had that appearance of being lonely or needful or whatever.... I would hunt them out." Another man commented that he looked mainly for "younger chicks ... young kinda girls" because the older ones were more "hip to your tricks." One father admitted that he was attracted more to his girlfriend's teenage daughter than to his girlfriend.

In terms of selecting a child victim, the majority of the men deliberately chose more physically developed children as they found them more desirable. Fewer men found a smaller, younger person more desirable. Several step-fathers recalled feeling sexually attracted to their step-daughters when they were pre-adolescents or adolescents and had begun to develop sexually. One step-father chose his victim based on her emerging adolescent sexuality and erroneous beliefs about her sexual availability. He explained how his role in the family changed from "father" to "abuser":

> I mean nothing sexual came [to me] about this girl until six months later ... after I moved in.... I wasn't, you know after her or anything at the time or right away.... I was just concerned about where she was going and that, like a father would be ... stuff like that. Then, uh, her mother told me that she got sexually assaulted by her father and you know, I felt sorry at the time and then that's when I started thinking like "Oh man, she's into sex!" stuff like that.... Then I started thinking, like "Oh wow, what would that be like to go with her?" and "She likes sex".... The most thing that really appealed to me was that I knew she was sexually active. That was the big thing.

Contact and Non-Contact Grooming Behaviours

The grooming process included both contact behaviours as well as non-contact behaviours. The more obvious grooming behaviours occurred through increased physical touching and body contact. One father took advantage of existing opportunities for desensitizing his daughter towards touching: "When she started swimming, she was competitively swimming and had trouble with her shoulders. That's where the massage came in." Another father stated, "At first it was me masturbating, then I started approaching, grooming ... like touching her head and touching her hand, you know holding her hand, stuff like that, petting her and stuff." Several fathers used affectionate touches, massages, tickling and physical contact games. Some fathers found the victims' weak points, which were usually their need for attention and affection. One father recounted,

> She was looking for affection and she was also lonely, but not to the point of sexual loneliness where I was. I'd hug her and hold her too long.... Every girl should get hugs from her father [pause] but not as long as I did.

Non-contact grooming included setting up situations in which abuse could occur and giving victims gifts and special privileges with the expectation that this "exchange" would eventually become mutual. One father commented: "If I'm rewarding my victim and making her feel good, then when I come to ask for something, I'm going to get it in return.... It was all manipulation and coercion." One step-father manipulated both the mother and the daughter by using drugs, money and alcohol:

> I used some of that money to get [um] sexual favours or even a
> kiss or a feel or whatever or have her watch me masturbate. I
> would give her maybe a gram of pot or whatever.… So I was
> using everything I can in order to get sexual favours from [the
> daughter].

The following scenario illustrates more subtle pre-offence intentions:

> I did things like … I'd go into the bathroom if she was in the
> shower.… Or she'd come into the bedroom after I'd showered.
> I'd leave the door—I wouldn't lock the door and I'd take a long
> time to dry off so if she came into the room, then she'd see me
> naked … by the time I was offending her I'm sure she had seen
> me naked, you know, a few times and that was part of my
> grooming.

Grooming also took the form of setting up situations for the opportunity to abuse. In most of the cases, the abuse took place in the family
home. Locating a time and place required thinking ahead: as one father
stated, "Timing was critical for me. I had to find the right time to
approach her which was mostly at night when everybody was in bed.
Lots of times she locked her door."

Some offenders used specific parenting styles to groom children
for later sexual compliance. Many fathers assumed an authoritarian
parenting style which focused on exerting power and control: "It was
my way or the highway. I was in control." In contrast, another father's
overly permissive parenting was a part of his grooming process:

> My kids never had curfews.… There was very little discipline.
> They came and went as they pleased. Uh, which had more to
> do with the fear of being found out than [laugh], you know …
> I was sexually abusing my children … that gave them licence to
> come and go as they pleased. I wasn't going to put my foot
> down on them. It's part of the control issue, isn't it—part of the
> rewards for allowing me to violate them was that they had
> freedom of movement.

Five fathers actively interfered with the mother-child relationships,
placing themselves in adversarial roles to the victims' mothers by
acting more as a friend to the children than as a parent—allowing extra
privileges and having the mothers administer the discipline.

Another common, subtle grooming pattern that emerged was discussing, or in some cases, *not* discussing sexuality issues. Talking to his
children about sex under the guise of educating them was a common

form of grooming behaviour for one man. One step-father initiated a discussion about the noises his step-daughter had heard from her mother's bedroom: "I said, 'Well that's your mom and I just making noises from an orgasm' and I asked her if she knew what it was and by this time I was already setting her up and playing her along." One father deliberately avoided discussing sexuality issues with his children,

> As for me talking to them about sexuality on real terms—NOT A CHANCE—never ... with any of them at any time ... because I had said nothing in the past, it was easy then to say "It's all right to do this ... because I'm your dad, would I hurt you?"

In another example, one step-father's desire to fit into his new family, as well as his cognitive distortions about sexuality and sex education, seemed to contribute to the sexual assault of his step-daughter:

> A thought came to mind that a woman will always love her first lover and first man. That's the old wives tale or whatever, and I believed that and at the time I was telling myself ... "Hey, if I can teach her how to have an orgasm...." Hey that's something you would share having done and I was telling myself that I was going to create this terrific bond.... I'd convince her that it's okay.

Thus, while some grooming behaviours could be distinctly identified, others were more subtle and manipulative. Grooming a child for sex for most of the offenders was a long and subtle process. One father summed it up: "Pretty much everything I did with that child, from the time she was ten years old on, was to have her manipulated and groomed and put in a position to succumb to what I want." The grooming process also did not appear to change much over time (or between abuse incidents), except, as one father stated, it often required "more liberties or larger rewards."

The Larger Context of Incest

In talking with these men it was readily apparent that there were many stresses in their lives. Varying degrees of childhood abuse, distrust, decreased emotional intimacy in relationships, pervasive feelings of insecurity, low self-esteem and worthlessness, and multiple job and family pressures were prevalent. These feelings and stressors caused the offenders to isolate themselves, adopt multiple addictions and to use their partners and/or daughters to meet their needs. Most of the perpetrators spent much of their lives suppressing their feelings and being emotionally shutdown. One man stated, "I was down quite often. Didn't recognize it, didn't feel it, didn't deal with it. And if you would ask me how things were going, most days I'd say, 'fine,' 'no problem' [laugh]."

Relationships with Female Partners, their Children and Women in General

The majority of the participants had emotionally distant and unhealthy relationships with their female partners and with women in general. Several offenders blamed their partners for their offending, saying that their partners were not fulfilling them sexually, were physically violent with the children, were verbally and physically abusive to the offender or were not available emotionally as a result of heavy drinking.

Some of the offending took place at a time when the men were emotionally estranged from their partners because of a fight, argument or separation. In many cases, the ability to control the mother facilitated the daughter's incest. One man said, "The mother was so easy to manipulate and whatever, I thought, 'I could get whatever I want from her.'" Another man explained,

> Three quarters of the time when we went out drinking, my wife wouldn't come home. Like, we'd go to dances.... What would happen is I'd want to go home early. "If you want to stay for the dance you stay. I'm going home.... I can't stand these people."... There's the grooming.... I knew [my step-daughter] would be at home [babysitting].

While the men were not directly asked whether the mothers had a history of childhood sexual abuse, four of the men were aware that their partners had been sexually abused as children. Six men said that their partners had previously been involved in an abusive relationship as adults and had problems with alcohol or drugs. Several of the men were violent towards their female partners; but, as with the incest, the violence was often minimized:

> I slapped her once. After that, I'd just walk away. Some people would say that that is abuse that I slapped her. I don't think ... like I never beat her up.... I take responsibility for slapping but I can't take responsibility for ever beating the shit out of her. Like, I'd never do that. I slapped her pretty hard and she got two black eyes.

Some of the men admitted they treated women like objects and manipulated them for their own gain. One man stated, "All my women that I dated, I was always using them for something—either money or sex." Another blamed his upbringing by saying, "I disrespected women. I don't know, maybe that comes from my childhood.... I've used women probably most of my life. I've used them as sex objects you know?" Several men lacked emotional intimacy and mixed it up with sexual gratification. One man said, "That was my attitude at the time. Sex is sex.... That was the goal. You know, you go out to the bar, you get drunk, you pick up a woman. That's the thing to do." Another stated,

> To me [sigh] what looked like love was sex in a sense. Affection had to do with sex I suppose ... like my father not only abused me sexually, uh, it didn't matter to him if my mother was knocked out or not, he would still have sex with her.

Several derogatory views about women emerged. One respondent distanced himself from the offence by consistently objectifying and referring to his ex-common-law spouse in the interview as "the mother" and his step-daughter as "the girl." Another man added, "The ones I wanted to marry, they dropped me and then I hated them—I hated women, I wanted to use them."

Many of the fathers described being emotionally and physically distanced from their children. They played a very limited role in their children's nurturing before and during the abuse. Several of the fathers felt less emotionally connected to their daughters. One man was proud of how he had raised his son; however, in reference to his daughter, whom he had been charged for offending against twice, he said, "I never had much to do with raising her. To teach her wisdom ... that wasn't my end of it. I was more interested in the boys."

Substance Abuse

Eleven of the thirteen men stated that alcohol and / or drugs played a role in their offending. They used substances to take away inhibitions before offending and to block out the memory of the offence. Many had begun abusing alcohol in their teenage years, and one man said he started drinking when he was eight years old. One father recognized that he relied on these substances to cope with his own history of abuse. Another father stated that he did not feel that he could have assaulted his daughter if he had not been under the influence of alcohol.

Family-of-Origin Issues

Witnessing and experiencing family violence was common for most men. One man stated, "All my life's been violent. My dad used to pay me and my brother to fight for him and his friends, and I didn't wanna, but my brother was bigger than me and I was small." Another man recalled, "When he came home drunk I would go out and hide out on the steps but I couldn't stay there because I would hear him arguing and fighting with my mom." All of the men described that, prior to therapy, they were unable to express their feelings. One man spoke of how his family background contributed to his views about women and his consequent inability to express feelings:

> It wasn't manly [to express feelings], you know. My dad was kind of a military man ... a very independent entrepreneur who expected men to be men and women to be women ... and uh, women had their role in life and men had their role in life and that's all there was to it.

Fantasies and Pornography

Some men admitted to using pornography as a sexual stimulus to offend. Fantasizing was often a part of the grooming process that led them to be sexual with their victims. One father admitted, "Absolutely there were fantasies.... When I was in the fantasy stage it was too late. My mind was set and it was going to happen ... and that was all there was to it." More than half of the men denied or did not recall fantasizing about their victim. Nine of the thirteen men had participated in activities that objectified women—watching strippers or looking at pornographic magazines or movies. One father frequented a sports bar, that had strippers, on a weekly basis. He struggled to connect this practice of seeing nude bodies to sexually assaulting his daughters.

Another father said that his offending behaviour provided him with closeness and affection and "it just seemed like that was the only return of affection that I could get." Later he said that he also received affection through viewing pornography: "It gave me affection back in a sense ... what I was missing with my wife." One father placed his offence within the larger scope of the problem of sexual violence when he said, "It doesn't just happen overnight. Pornography, hookers, [pause] the cycle just ... from one to another, to another to another, drugs and pretty soon you find yourself in this great big vacuum and there's nothing you can do."

Issues of Power and Control

Themes of power and control in the family, in the workplace and in manipulating child victims and spouses were prevalent. Many men spoke of the importance of being in complete control over their lives and over the people around them. One father denied that he used any grooming because his daughter (and family) were afraid of him and would do what he said. Another man spoke about his wife, "I was so jealous of her, so if I get her knocked up, then she's stuck with me, you see? There was no love there. I think I wanted to own her."

A biological father, separated from his wife at the time of the assaults, struggled with whether his motivation to assault his daughters was for sex or for affection. His statement clearly suggested other factors—control, revenge towards his ex-wife and anger.

> I love my daughters, I had affection for them but it wasn't a sexual attraction. Then, there must have been a sexual attraction towards them to kiss their vaginas. It still comes down to that. And I'm still at grips with that and going, "Was it really a sexual attraction or was it simply a sign of affection?" … When I look at it now thinking back, to do it, to be closer to them than their mother … nobody else would do this…. They were my possessions…. And because of that you can lose tremendous amounts [sigh].

Views of Masculinity and Fatherhood

The majority of the men subscribed to traditional notions of a male's role in society and in the family. This included strongly emphasizing work and financial success, having difficulty expressing their feelings, supporting rigid sex roles in the family and discomfort with the father role. Nearly every participant called himself a workaholic. Others described patterns that reflected an unhealthy balance among work, leisure and family. Many men saw their supportive role in the family primarily as bread earners and providers. One man stated, "I was totally aware that I was useless. Just a paycheck." This comment by another man is also strikingly common among many non-offenders today:

> I was going to get ahead. I was going to retire a millionaire at thirty-eight and that's all there was to it, and I knew what I had to do to do it. I was gonna follow dad's footsteps and I was gonna make it there and I had big expectations of myself.

Many men recognized that they could not easily trust others or open up emotionally to their wives or partners. One man described his lack of emotional expression in his relationships, "I guess I was afraid to … not you know, appear masculine and, 'boys don't cry' and 'boys don't hurt and men don't cry and men don't hurt.'" Another man admitted, "Even my loneliness or my hurt or my anger or anything … like, that was all kept inside of me. I didn't let anybody know about it. I put a front mask…. I camouflaged all of it. That was hard."

Several men held rigid views on the roles of women and men in the family. One man said:

She did anything that I wanted. Like, she was there to basically to please me. She never worked. She never had to because I worked and I worked long hours. I made lots of money.... I thought a wife should have been there. It was her duty, you know, to have sex with me and stuff.

While some men felt extremely competent in their workplaces, other men felt much less competent as husbands or parents: "I was very ... confident in terms of business ... where I could be in control, the authority figure ... but, in an intimate relationship, not a chance. I had no idea how to do it. None whatsoever."

Several step-fathers' comments revealed the uncertainty of their role as a parent to their step-children. This apparent role confusion was evident in comments such as, "I'll have no authority" and "I have no control and I know the thought was there of, 'Will I ever be accepted?' I know I wanted to be called 'Dad.'" Two step-fathers explicitly suggested to the mother that they should have a sexual relationship with the daughter. One step-father, whose wife had several miscarriages, had concerns about her ability to carry a child to term. He never had any sons, yet wanted one. His comment highlights his distortion of the legal and biological aspects of the father-daughter relationship: "I remember telling my wife one time ... I said you know, L. is only my step-daughter, if I got her pregnant and she had a son, my son ... that wouldn't be that bad, 'cause she's only my step-daughter."

Implications
Grooming Behaviours
What these men have said regarding the process used by incest offenders in preparing to sexually abuse their victims raises a number of prevention and treatment issues for offenders and their families. While the majority of men minimized and denied using grooming behaviours, perhaps due to their desire to appear in a positive light in the interview, they did identify a variety of grooming behaviours. Although many of the behaviours they described may be present in families where there is no incest, grooming behaviours are distinguished from normal parenting behaviours because they are premeditated, deliberate steps taken with the intention to offend.

It is critical to examine the subtle manipulative and controlling behaviours of sex offenders towards all family members, not just the incest victim. This occurs when the perpetrator purposely undermines the mother's role with her children, often through physically abusing and intimidating her. It may be startling that the majority of grooming behaviours and incest offences took place inside the family home; this is not surprising, however, considering the extent to which offenders normalized sexually abusive activities and manipulated the child victims and the mothers. Mothers whose children have been sexually abused often experience feelings of guilt, blame and responsibility for their child's abuse. Some mothers may also worry about their ability to select safe partners. Connecting numerous offender patterns with specific grooming behaviours and control strategies may help non-offending mothers who are in therapy decrease self-blame.

Identification of grooming behaviours can assist family members and help professionals outside the family to identify potentially risky situations and inappropriate interactions that may lead to the occurrence or continuation of sexual abuse. It is worth noting, however, that many perpetrators use subtlety and sophistication to disguise their grooming behaviours as normal caregiving activities: this may make it difficult for adults, let alone child victims themselves, to identify these situations.

A commonly used treatment model with sex offenders is the relapse prevention model. This model assumes that sexual offences are consciously planned and teaches offenders to recognize the precursors to their offending behaviour by defining their own offence cycle. Identifying the variety of offender grooming behaviours is important in helping offenders break through the denial involved in asserting that the molestation "just happened." This process can also enable offenders to recognize that they have the ability to control and change their behavior before committing the offence. One participant brought to the interview his own offence cycle which he had previously mapped out with his counsellor. He said that it was only through his work in therapy that he was able to identify the grooming behaviours he used with his daughter.

Contextual Factors

Larger contextual factors play a significant role in incest offences, even though few men connected their offending behaviour to these larger factors. Most men minimized the effects of their own past abuse, job stress and exposure to pornography in assaulting their daughters. Many attributed their offending to the use of alcohol and/or drugs. Some men, however, were more insightful, and, with the help of treatment, recognized these other causal factors.

The men generally had poor marital relationships and held negative views about women. Addressing the view of women and children as sex objects is imperative in the prevention of incestuous victimization and in the treatment of offenders. In changing offender behaviour, it is often necessary for offenders to re-examine and modify their core beliefs and attitudes about men and women. As a society we need to identify the dominant messages which sexualize women and children and reconsider ways in which people are socialized into gender roles. Men need to be encouraged to depart from the dominant ideologies of gender: as long as boys and men are socialized to exercise power and control over their environment and others, to separate themselves emotionally from others, to suppress emotions that are culturally defined as non-masculine, to minimize the importance of their role as nurturing parents and to succumb to gendered notions of what men are "supposed to be," our society will always have the problem of incest.

For most of the men, incest revolved around cognitive distortions and the inability to handle life stresses in healthy ways (e.g., communicating with their partner, decreasing their workload). Instead of dealing with their feelings, these men submerged themselves in work, isolated themselves emotionally or relied on alcohol or drugs. They compensated for feelings of inadequacy through controlling their victims and the non-offending spouse. Men need to be provided with alternative, non-sexual and non-violent ways of dealing directly with stress and painful emotions.

Successful relapse prevention requires that offenders learn victim empathy, get in touch with their feelings and overcome denial and rationalizations. Many of the men became sexual with their daughters in order to feel emotionally closer to them, confusing affection with sex. Instead of verbalizing their emotions, the men acted out their feelings in a sexually violent fashion. Incest offenders need to understand and address in therapy the feelings that trigger them to act out sexually with their child.

There appear to be several contextual factors within the family that may make children more vulnerable to being incestuously abused. Since parents often perceive their younger children to be most vulnerable to victimization, they tend to be more protective of them. However, most offenders in this study stated that they began to perceive their daughters as more sexually appealing and available when their daughters or step-daughters began developing sexually physically and engaging in typical adolescent behaviours such as dating and drinking. One step-father claimed that his step-daughter was "into sex" and that "female children become sexual beings once they show sexual behaviour." This finding suggests that older preadolescent and adolescent female children may be at an increased risk for abuse by paternal incest offenders.

Increased vulnerability to committing abuse appears to be partly due to offenders' rationalizations about child sexuality. Thus, for example, children's prior history of sexual victimization may also make them more vulnerable to further victimization. Recall the step-father who revealed that knowing his step-daughter had been sexually abused made her a more attractive target to him and, in his words, gave him a "green light" to be sexual with her. Immediate intervention with child victims of sexual abuse is imperative to avoid further victimization and to minimize child victim blaming in cases where the child displays inappropriate provocative behaviour due to past sexual victimization.

The majority of the men had little involvement in their children's caregiving. Step-fathers especially may face a difficult task. Several step-fathers in this study spoke of being uncertain about their parental role. Blurred generational boundaries and role confusion are more pronounced for step-fathers and mothers' boyfriends; this may increase the risk of, and the father's vulnerability towards, offending behaviour (Faller 1990). Unfortunately, due to the small number of stepfathers interviewed, we must be cautious in drawing such conclusions. Further research needs to examine incest offenders' perceived role as fathers, specifically focusing on their emotional attachment to their children. It may also be useful to distinguish among biological, legal and non-legal relationships between fathers and their children.

Conclusion

This exploratory study identified specific grooming behaviours of incest offenders. It showed how father-daughter incest is a deliberately planned process that often involves contact and non-contact behaviours. The offenders in this study explicitly described how they selected and prepared their victims and set up the offence. This research also provides insight into the societal influences that shape the attitudes and perceptions of offenders; it shows that one must look beyond the specific grooming behaviours to the various family and societal contexts.

We cannot remove sexually violent acts from their social context. There remains a pressing need in current research to consider how social factors influence offender thinking and grooming behaviours. Both women and men must continue to tell their stories about their experiences of violence (either as victims or perpetrators) in order to more fully understand how violence is an ingrained key component of our culture.

Chapter 5

Court Processing of Child Sexual Abuse Cases
The Winnipeg Family Violence Court Experience[1]
Jane Ursel and Kelly Gorkoff

Introduction

Those who have worked with abused children or have sat through trials in which children are called upon to testify about their abuse know how little of the terrible story statistics tell. In one sense, these cold, orderly numbers do no service to these children. No numbers can capture their complex and compelling stories … the betrayals of trust, the deep psychological damage, the struggle to heal. However, those who have lobbied for change to expand supportive programs and alter existing systems, know that these numbers are essential. We need these numbers to demonstrate that the sum of these very personal tragedies signifies a major social problem. The struggle for social justice calls for the powerful stories of individuals to capture the hearts and secure the commitment of policy-makers. We also need the numbers, as evidence of the magnitude of the problem, to capture the attention of the Treasury Board. This chapter is a small contribution to the consideration of a large social problem. It is our hope that insight into how one criminal justice system works may help to improve it and may help others design better systems.

The National Background

In Canada, child abuse has been recognized as a problem requiring state intervention since the first child protection legislation was passed in Ontario in 1893 (Ursel 1992a). Public responsibility to protect children is embodied in the Criminal Code of Canada and provincial child welfare legislation. For the most part, child welfare agencies have been the primary intervener in situations of child abuse. However, in the

79

past twenty years there have been a series of shocking revelations of child sexual abuse which have led to greater involvement of the criminal justice system. As a result of growing public awareness of the prevalence of child sexual abuse, significant changes have been made to provincial child welfare statutes and to the Criminal Code to provide greater protection to children at risk (Young 1992).

In December 1980, the Canadian Parliament established the "Committee on Sexual Offences Against Children and Youth." The report of this Committee (the Badgley Report 1984) put a strong emphasis on the need to invoke criminal sanctions for offenders, for both deterrence and rehabilitation purposes (Wells 1990). Acting on the recommendations of the Badgley Report, Parliament passed *An Act to Amend the Criminal Code and the Canada Evidence Act as it Pertains to Children* (formerly Bill C-15), which was enacted on January 1, 1988. This Act had four broad goals: (1) to provide better protection to child sexual abuse victims; (2) to enhance successful prosecution of child sexual abuse cases; (3) to improve the experience of the child victim/witness and (4) to bring sentencing in line with the severity of the offence. The legislation expanded the opportunities for courts to receive children's testimony and introduced several new sexual offences against children including sexual interference, sexual exploitation and invitation to sexual touching.

The sexual abuse provisions of this legislation have significantly reduced impediments to the criminal justice prosecution of child abuse cases. Studies of the impact of these provisions were conducted in Hamilton-Wentworth and Toronto (Campbell Research Associates 1992a, 1992b), in Regina and Saskatoon (Stevens, Fischer & Berg 1992) and in Edmonton and Calgary (Hornick, Burrows, Perry & Bolitho 1992). All studies showed some changes in practice, ranging from increased services for child witnesses in the Hamilton-Wentworth district to increased laying of charges and convictions in Saskatchewan. The purpose of this chapter is to add to the small but growing number of studies on the criminal prosecution of child sexual abuse cases. Winnipeg provides a particularly interesting case study because of the specialization that has occurred in our criminal justice system to respond to family violence cases.

The Winnipeg Family Violence Court

Concurrent with growing national attention and action with respect to child abuse offences, the Manitoba Department of Justice developed a unique response to the general issue of family violence. In September of 1990 a specialized family violence criminal court was introduced. The implementation of the Family Violence Court (FVC) represented an institutional recognition of the special needs of victims who are in "a relationship of trust, dependency and/or kinship" with their alleged offender. Because it is presumed that all children are in a relationship of trust and/or dependency with all adults, all child abuse prosecutions in which the accused is an adult come before this court.

Components of this specialized system which are of particular importance in child abuse prosecutions are: (1) a child abuse investigation unit within the Winnipeg Police Service; (2) a child victim/witness advocacy program within the Department of Justice; (3) eleven specialized Crown attorneys; (4) specially designated courtrooms and dockets for intake, screening court and trials and (5) the recent construction of a "child friendly" courtroom to be utilized for child abuse prosecutions.

Between 1990 and 1997 the Family Violence Court dealt with 23,009 family violence cases: 89 percent were spousal abuse cases, 10 percent were child abuse cases and 1 percent were elder abuse cases. The existence of the specialized court has enhanced our ability to identify and track family violence cases through the court system.[2] This chapter will present a descriptive summary of the child sexual abuse cases that have come before the FVC for the five-year period from 1992 to 1997.[3] We will make some comparisons with national data and consider the difference in court outcomes between cases involving alleged physical abuse versus those involving alleged sexual abuse.

The incidence of child abuse in our community is much greater than criminal court statistics alone would suggest. In Winnipeg, about one-third or less of the reported cases of child abuse proceed through criminal court. The majority of cases are dealt with through child welfare interventions (Ursel 1992b). The predominance of civil remedies reflects the fact that it is less onerous to prove abuse or neglect in a civil case because the standard of proof is based on the balance of probabilities. In criminal court the onus is on the prosecution to prove its case beyond a reasonable doubt—the highest legal standard of proof. As a result, Crown attorneys carefully review their cases, proceeding to trial only when they believe they have sufficient evidence (including a strong enough witness) to be able to meet the more rigorous standard of proof in criminal court. Thus the cases we see in FVC are merely the tip of the iceberg.

Child Abuse Prosecutions—Case Characteristics

For the purposes of this discussion, "child abuse" includes cases in which the victim was under age eighteen and the accused was an adult. There are also a limited number of historical abuse cases (52) included in this data set. These are cases in which an adult makes a complaint about her/his sexual abuse as a child. This data set does not include cases in which children are assaulted by youth, as these cases are heard in Youth Court.

Gender, Age and Abuse

Between 1992 and 1997, 1,349 cases of child abuse came before the Winnipeg FVC. Forty-five percent (604) were cases of sexual abuse, while 55 percent (745) were cases of physical abuse. For all types of abuse, the majority of the victims were female (83 percent), while the majority of the accused were men (91 percent). The gendered nature of the crime is equally pronounced in cases of sexual abuse, in which 83 percent (726) of the victims were girls, and 97 (587) percent of the accused were men.

The Winnipeg court data are consistent with prior child sexual abuse research which indicated that the majority of child sexual abuse victims are female. For example, the Badgley Report (1984) found that 78 percent of the victims under age sixteen were girls. The Department of Justice study in 1992 reported that 83 percent of the victims were girls (Bisenthal & Clement 1992: 6). The research to evaluate the child sexual abuse legislation found that 70 to 80 percent of the victims in the site studies were female (Hornick & Bolitho 1992: 105). Compared to this research, the Winnipeg data report a higher concentration of girl victims (varying from 5 to 12 percent higher, depending on the study). This may be a function of our data source, as the Winnipeg study includes the whole population of cases, while the other studies involved different sampling procedures.

The Winnipeg court data suggest another gender-based difference. A girl's vulnerability to abuse appears to increase with age, while a boy's vulnerability appears to decrease with age. When we consider all cases of abuse, 77 percent of the incidents involving girl victims occur at the age of twelve years or older, while 57 percent of the incidents involving boy victims occur at the age of eleven years or younger. This reverse pattern of age and gender continues with sexual abuse cases; however, it is not as pronounced. When we consider sexual abuse cases (see Table 1), 62 percent of incidents involving girl victims occur at the age of twleve years or older, while 51 percent of the incidents involving boy victims occur at the age of eleven years or younger. These data suggest that the onset of puberty carries special risks for girl children. However, we must also consider the possibility that it may reflect different patterns of disclosure among boys and girls by age. Some practitioners have suggested that as boys get older they are less likely to disclose their abuse.

The age of the victims in the sexual abuse cases reviewed ranged from one to seventeen years, with the average age being twelve years. The age of the accused in these cases ranged from eighteen to eighty-seven years, with the average age being thirty-four years. The single measure of age highlights the substantial power differential between the victim and the accused.

Table 1
Child Sexual Abuse Cases by Victim's Age and Gender
Winnipeg Family Violence Court 1992–1997*

| | Female Victim | | Male Victim | |
| | N = 564 | | N = 86 | |
	Number	Percent	Number	Percent
Age 5 and under	41	7%	11	13%—
				51%
6–11 years	172	30%	33	38%—
12–14 years	191	33%—	20	24%
		62%		
15–17 years	160	29%—	22	27%

* Seventy-nine (73 female and 6 male) historical abuse cases are not included in this table. Sixty male and female cases are also not included due to the fact that we cannot match up age to sex of victim for male and female victim cases. Also, since we record age for the first three victims only, there is no age for twenty-nine female victims.

Nature of Relationship between Victim and Accused
Another factor speaking to the power dynamics between the victim and the accused is the nature of the relationship. Twenty-four percent of all victims were abused by a parent (biological, foster or step-parent), in all cases clearly a person in authority. Eighteen percent were abused by other family members (grandparent, uncle/aunt or brother/sister). Thus intrafamilial[4] abuse is the single largest category, accounting for 42 percent of the incidents. The remainder of cases included abuse by an acquaintance/neighbour (21 percent), friend (10 percent), stranger (8 percent), intimate relation (boyfriend/girlfriend, common-law, etc.—4 percent), caregiver (3 percent) and other (12 percent).

Duration of Abuse
As to the duration of abuse, approximately one-half of the cases heard in FVC involved single incidents (49 percent). The length of abuse in the remainder of cases was 1 to 5 months (14 percent), 6 to 12 months (8 percent), 13 to 24 months (7 percent), 25 to 36 months (6 percent) and more than 3 years (16 percent). Although Gordon (1990) reported that girls are much more likely than boys to experience repeated abuse, our data do not indicate a significant difference in the duration of abuse for boy or girl victims.

Single incident abuse cases account for 50 percent of the girl victims and 48 percent of the boy victims. Of those cases in which the duration of abuse was over two years, 22 percent involved girl victims and 18 percent involved boys. The one category which had the highest concentration of long-term abuse was that involving multiple victims who were boys and girls (27 cases). Half of these cases involved abuse over two years in duration.

Ethnic Background

When we consider ethnic background,[5] we find that 59 percent of the accused and 55 percent of the victims are of European origin, 15 percent of the accused and 14 percent of the victims are "visible minorities" and 26 percent of the accused and 31 percent of the victims are of Aboriginal origin. In a city in which 10 percent of the population is of Aboriginal origin, Aboriginal victims and offenders are overrepresented. The Winnipeg court data are consistent with national studies in the United States and Canada, which report that child sexual abuse is a particular concern for Aboriginal people. In general, Aboriginal people are overrepresented as victims of abuse and Aboriginal girls are sexually victimized in greater numbers than Aboriginal boys (McEvoy & Daniluk 1995; Robin et al. 1997). The Ontario Native Women's Association (1989) found that eight in ten Aboriginal women have been victims of sexual assault at some point in their lives. A study commissioned by the Correctional Service of Canada (1996) found that Aboriginal females are the prime target of Aboriginal sex offenders. The same report revealed that up to 75 percent of victims are females under age eighteen, 50 percent are under age fourteen and almost 25 percent are younger than age seven.

Additional Offences

In 1988, the Criminal Code amendments created new categories of sexual offences against children, including sexual interference, sexual exploitation and invitation to sexual touching. Table 2 presents the list of major charge categories in the FVC relating to sexual abuse cases. The data suggest that the police are making substantial use of the new charges with sexual interference and invitation to sexual touching being the second and third most frequently laid charges. The most frequently laid charge is sexual assault.

Prior Record

A final observation on case characteristics relates to the prior record of the accused (see Table 3). It is a sobering fact that 66 percent of the accused in these cases had a prior record. Further, of those who had a prior record, 65 percent had a record including another "crime against persons." The most common prior crime against persons was sexual assault (34 percent). Interestingly, in only three cases the prior record was related to child abuse. This high prior record rate suggests that the accused in these cases are dangerous individuals. The high incidence of prior assaults is an important factor for practitioners to consider in the development of treatment plans.

Table 2
Child Sexual Abuse: Major Charge Categories
Winnipeg Family Violence Court 1992–1997
N = 604

Charge	Counts**	Number of Cases with Charge	Percent of Cases with Charge
Sexual Assault	659	494	82%
Sexual Interference	450	341	56%
Invitation to Sexual Touching	141	113	19%
Sexual Exploitation	63	49	8%
Violent Assault*	45	29	5%

* Includes charges: Assault with a Weapon, Aggravated Assault, Assault Causing Bodily Harm, Sexual Assault Threats/Bodily Harm/Weapon and Aggravated Sexual Assault.
** Counts indicate the number of times the charge appears, e.g., one accused can be charged on three incidents against the same victim and thus be charged with three counts of sexual assault.

Table 3
Prior Record: Child Sexual Abuse Cases
Winnipeg Family Violence Court 1992–1997
N = 360

	Number of Cases	Percent of Cases
Type of Prior Record	360	66%
Domestic	40	11%
General Assault	70	19%
Child Abuse	3	.01%
Sexual Abuse	122	34%
All Crimes against Person	235	65%
Other Record	125	35%

Case Outcomes

In this section we will: (1) consider the length of time involved in court processing; (2) describe the disposition of sexual abuse prosecutions; (3) identify the consistent differences in case outcome between sexual abuse and physical abuse cases in the Winnipeg FVC and (4) compare the case outcomes in FVC with national data, where possible. An overview of case outcomes is contained in Figure 1.

An important aspect of the criminal prosecution of child sexual abuse is the length of time involved. While a case proceeds through the courts, the child and the supportive family members experience significant emotional turmoil. In order to preserve the integrity of the evidence, parents are sometimes advised not to discuss the case with their child, and sometimes a child may forgo counselling in order to avoid creating a record that could be subpoenaed by the defence. Thus, the longer the court process, the longer it takes to begin the healing. In recognition of this fact, one of the goals of the specialized court was to expedite these cases.

Figure 1 indicates that 242, or 58 percent, of the cases that proceeded to court involved guilty pleas, and 174, or 42 percent, involved trials. Table 4 identifies the length of time that cases were before the courts by the plea of the accused. Overall the average length of time for trials was one year, and guilty pleas were disposed more rapidly. While there are cases that are complicated by appeals and procedural delays that may extend the process over three years, these cases are the exception.

Specialization permits court staff to keep track of upcoming cases and free up courtrooms for child abuse trials. Unfortunately we do not have any data prior to specialization to determine the magnitude of its impact on processing time. However, we do know that with specialization a number of courtrooms were designated for child abuse hearings and every effort is made to utilize additional courtrooms if there is any indication of delay.

In considering overall outcome, interesting differences emerge between physical and sexual abuse cases within Winnipeg and between the Winnipeg data and the national data. First, our data indicate that through all stages of the court process, sexual abuse was treated as a more serious offence than physical abuse. These indicators are:

- a greater percentage of physical abuse cases (37 percent) were stayed compared to 31 percent of the sexual abuse cases.
- twice as many sexual abuse cases (29 percent) go to trial than physical abuse cases (13 percent).
- a greater percentage of accused in sexual abuse cases (50 percent) are found guilty at trial compared to 39 percent of accused in physical abuse cases.

Figure 1 — Child Sexual Abuse Cases*
Winnipeg Family Violence Court 1992–1997

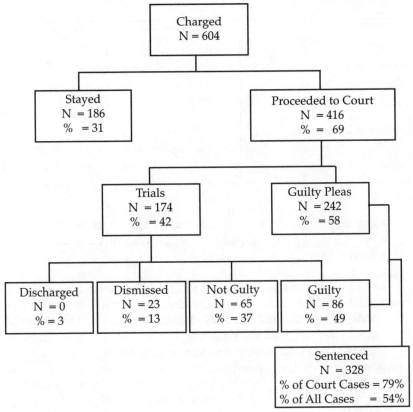

* 2 Accused deceased

Table 4
Court Processing Time by Plea
Winnipeg Family Violence Court 1992–1997

Court Processing Time	Guilty Plea	Trial
	N = 242	N = 174
6 months or less	56%	16%
7–12 months	29%	40%
13–18 months	9%	32%
19 months and over	6%	13%

Table 5
Case Outcome in Child Sexual Abuse Cases
Winnipeg and National Data

Outcome	National Data (ACCS) N = 2060	Winnipeg Data N = 604
Conviction	46%	54%
Stayed	13%	31%
Acquitted, Discharged, Withdrawn	34%	15%
Other	7%	–

- a greater percentage of those accused of physical abuse (50 percent) enter a guilty plea compared to 40 percent of those accused of sexual abuse.

The national data base[6] used for comparison with the Winnipeg court data is taken from the Adult Criminal Court Survey (ACCS) (Bisenthal & Clement 1992: 51). Table 5 compares the court outcomes of the national data set with the Winnipeg Family Violence Court data.

There are two notable differences between Winnipeg and national outcomes. In Winnipeg, there was a significantly higher conviction rate. It is hoped that the higher conviction rate reflects the benefits gained by specialization of the criminal justice system in Winnipeg. However, given that we do not have access to the complete national data set in order to do detailed control tests, we can only speculate that specialization is a factor in the difference. The second difference is simply an artifact of the categories for non-conviction. While our "stay" rate seems much higher, this is a function of including withdrawn cases in the "stay" category, while the national data include them in the acquitted and discharged category. Overall, 46 percent of the Winnipeg cases and 54 percent of the national cases resulted in no conviction.

In summary, case outcome measures indicate that the specialized criminal justice system in Winnipeg treats sexual abuse cases more seriously than physical abuse cases and appears to have a higher conviction rate than other courts throughout the country.

Sentencing

The pattern of differences revealed above are similarly evident when we examine sentencing. Table 6 compares sentencing of child sexual abuse and physical abuse cases in Winnipeg courts with national sexual abuse sentencing data.

The most dramatic difference between the two types of cases is found in the incarceration rate. Within Winnipeg, persons convicted of child sexual abuse were more than twice as likely to get a sentence of incarceration (63 percent) than persons convicted of physical abuse (25 percent). Across jurisdictions we find that a greater percentage of persons convicted of sexual abuse in Winnipeg receive a jail sentence (63 percent) compared to 54 percent of sexual abuse offenders nationwide. In addition, our Winnipeg data indicate that for sexual abuse offenders, guilty verdicts dramatically increase the likelihood of a jail sentence (80 percent) over guilty pleas (63 percent). For physical abuse offenders the discrepancy in sentence between a guilty verdict and a guilty plea is minimal (34 percent and 33 percent respectively).

While incarceration itself is an important measure of court censure of child abuse offenders, an equally important measure is the length of incarceration to which the offender is sentenced. Table 7 indicates the difference in length of sentence for child physical and child sexual abuse offenders in the Winnipeg courts.

While 37 percent of sexual abuse offenders received a sentence of two years or more, only 6 percent of the physical abuse offenders received such a sentence within the Winnipeg courts. This indicates that sexual abuse is treated as a more serious offence meriting a longer sentence than physical abuse. Nationally, 94 percent of the sexual abuse offenders who were sentenced to incarceration received a sentence of

Table 6
Sentencing by Type of Child Abuse Case
and by Jurisdiction of Court*

	Child Sexual Abuse National Data N = 2060	Child Sexual Abuse Cases Winnipeg** N = 604	Child Physical Abuse Cases Winnipeg N = 745
Total Convictions	46%	54%	55%
Incarceration	54%	63%	25%
Probation	41%	30%	57%
Fine	4%	6%	13%
Other	1%	9%	18%

* Percentages based on total cases convicted
** Percentages are greater than 100 in the Winnipeg data set because the offender frequently receives multiple sentences, i.e., fine and probation or incarceration and probation.

Table 7
Length of Jail Sentence by Type of Child Abuse
Winnipeg Family Violence Court 1992–1997
N = 280

Time	Sexual Abuse Cases N = 183*		Physical Abuse Cases N = 96**	
	Number	Percent	Number	Percent
1–3 months	61	33%	57	59%
4–6 months	21	11%	18	19%
7–11 months	8	4%	7	7%
12 months	11	6%	3	3%
18 months	15	8%	5	5%
Provincial Institutions	116	63%	90	94%
2 years	18	10%	2	2%
3 years	19	10%	2	2%
4 years	12	7%	1	1%
5 years+	18	10%	1	1%
Federal Institutions	67	37%	6	6%

* No information on length of sentence for eight cases.
** No information on length of sentence for seven cases. Percentages greater than 100 due to rounding off.

less than two years, with 6 percent receiving more than two years incarceration. In comparison, there is a fivefold difference, with Winnipeg courts sentencing 37 percent of offenders to two years or more.

Lest we think that all Winnipeg judges are unusually harsh in sentencing, it is instructive to note that the suggested starting point in case law for sentencing child sexual abuse offenders is four years.[7] However, in only 30 child sexual abuse cases (or 17 percent) were offenders sentenced to four or more years. One is curious about what distinguishes these 30 cases. They do have some very distinctive characteristics, including: (1) 43 percent involved abuse longer than three years in duration, (2) 46 percent involved multiple victims, (3) 50 percent involved parent offenders, (4) 43 percent involved children under age 12 and (5) 70 percent involved multiple counts and multiple charges.

While length of incarceration is not the only important factor in assessing criminal justice outcomes, it is interesting that only 17 percent of child sexual abuse offenders were sentenced in accordance with the starting point suggested in case law. This may suggest that one of the goals of the child sexual abuse amendments to the Criminal Code, "to bring sentencing in line with the severity of the crime," may be more difficult to achieve.

At the other end of the continuum of consequences are those offenders who received the least severe sentences. Typically, fines and conditional sentences (i.e., incarceration sentences not served in an institution)[8] are viewed as the least severe consequences. In the FVC case, although fines and conditional sentences do occur, they seldom occur as the sole sentence but rather as one component in a combination of sentencing outcomes. Of the 328 convicted offenders, 21 received fines and 14 conditional sentences. All of the offenders who were fined also received a probation sentence and one offender received a fine, probation and a three-month sentence of intermittent incarceration. This pattern is similar in cases receiving conditional sentences. Of the 14 offenders who had a conditional sentence, 11 were also sentenced to a term of probation and one offender received a sentence of incarceration and probation as well as a conditional sentence. Only two of the offenders received a conditional sentence alone. In one case a forty-year-old white male was charged with "procuring juvenile prostitution" involving four juvenile Aboriginal girl victims. In the other case, it was one count of sexual interference and one count of sexual assault involving a forty-year-old white male who was an "acquaintance" of the six-year-old girl victim. In both cases the offender pled guilty and the offences involved a single incident.

To date it appears that lenient sentences are rare in the conviction of child sexual abuse offenders in the Winnipeg courts. Typically fines and conditional sentences exist as components in a multiple sentence outcome. However, the two cases in which conditional sentences were the sole consequence for the offender are cause for concern and suggest a close analysis of future cases to determine how this new sentencing option will be applied over time.

Conclusion

The decision to proceed through the criminal justice system with a child sexual abuse case is not taken lightly. The implications for the child victim/witness are significant. While the case proceeds through the courts, the matter stays alive and fresh in the child's psyche. If the child is called upon to testify, the telling of her/his story in court and the process of cross examination are daunting experiences. However, society has determined that the nature of the crime is so serious that criminal justice intervention is necessary. The balancing of a "child's best interest" against the need for formal justice intervention is very delicate. In Winnipeg, we know that the Crown attorneys exercise this discretion very seriously: less than a third of the child sexual abuse investigations result in the laying of a criminal charge.

A number of changes were made with the child sexual abuse amendments in 1988 to try to minimize the distress to the child and to enhance the probability of conviction. It is clear that the new categories of offences for child sexual abuse are being well-utilized by investigating officers. In 56 percent of all the child sexual abuse cases in FVC the charge was of sexual interference; 19 percent involved the charge of invitation to sexual touching. In addition, the Manitoba Department of Justice has introduced specialization within the criminal justice system because of its belief that victims in a relationship of trust, dependency and/or kinship with the accused have special needs and face special challenges.

Specialization of the criminal justice system in Winnipeg plays an important role in balancing the child's best interests with the interest of criminal court intervention. Specialization ensures that the same prosecutor stays with the case until it is disposed. It also provides a core group of peers for prosecutors who work in this field, who struggle with the same issues and who provide an important reference group when hard decisions need to be made. Specialization creates a new culture of prosecution which encourages crown attorneys to be aware of, and attend to, the special needs of their vulnerable witnesses. While these benefits of specialization are hard to quantify, their advantages for the child witness are readily apparent.

A number of issues arise from our analysis that have policy and program implications beyond the courtroom. The overrepresentation of Aboriginal children as victims of sexual assaults speaks to the importance of culturally specific programming for victims, supportive family members and offenders. As we write this chapter, Manitoba is in the process of mandating Aboriginal and Metis child welfare agencies with the enforcement of child welfare legislation throughout the province. Clearly the sexual victimization of Aboriginal children calls for special attention as the mandate is extended.

The inverse relationship between age, gender and child sexual abuse identified in Table 1 merits further research. The pattern revealed in the court data suggests that girls' vulnerability to abuse increases with age, while boys' vulnerability decreases. Is this peculiar to cases selected for criminal prosecution? Is the pattern an artifact of reporting behaviour? Does this pattern emerge in cases involving child welfare interventions? These questions are important to educators and practitioners, who play a critical role in reporting abuse and treating victims and their family members.

Finally, the sentencing reforms introduced in 1996, which created the option of conditional sentencing, are only captured in the last year of our data set. While the 1997 data suggest a very moderate application of such a lenient sentence in the Winnipeg courts, it will be important to follow the use of this sentence over time. In a similar vein, the 1997 Supreme Court decision that overruled the "starting point" concept in case law falls outside the parameters of our study. However, it will be very important to compare sentencing in subsequent years to determine whether such a decision will result in a pattern of more lenient sentences and undermine the intention of the 1988 Criminal Code amendments "to bring sentencing in line with the severity of the crime."

The balancing of the child's best interest against the need for formal justice intervention is a very serious responsibility that largely falls on the shoulders of our Crown prosecutors. We believe that all the information and research on the implications of criminal prosecutions of child abuse cases needs to be readily available to inform their decision making.

Notes

1. We would like to acknowledge the support of the Social Sciences and Humanities Research Council Strategic Grants Program "Women and Change" which provided funding to conduct this research in 1993–94 and 1995. We would also like to acknowledge the support of the Manitoba Department of Justice which is funding us to collect court data in subsequent years. Further, a special thank you to Dianne Bulback for her hours of work formatting tables, charts and editing our work.

2. The data presented in this chapter come from a larger "court tracking project," which began with the introduction of FVC and records all cases allocated to FVC. Information is collected at two points in time. The first point is at court intake: all cases on the intake docket are entered on a case management system, which provides our list and identifying characteristics of the cases before the FVC court in a one-year period. At the end of each year we begin a new list. As cases are disposed we use the completed crown attorney's case file to code case characteristics and court processing information, including verdict and sentence for each case. It frequently takes up to two years to complete a one-year intake due to case appeals, locating accused who are out on warrant and procedural delays. Overall we are able to code data on approximately 94 percent of all the cases that enter the system. The missing six percent are typically the result of cases still out on warrant, cases where the accused died and a small number of cases that could not be found.

3. While all child abuse cases first appear in FVC, approximately 25 percent of the cases, typically the most serious cases, are heard in Court of Queen's

Bench. These cases are included in our data set.

4. For the purposes of this chapter intrafamilial is defined as a person in a parenting role, either biological, foster or step-parent, and other relatives (e.g., grandparent, aunt or uncle).

5. While we acknowledge that ethnic status is a difficult matter to measure, we decided that collecting this information, as imperfect as it is, was preferable to having no information on ethnic background at all. Our information on ethnic identification comes from police and court files and is often based on police or self-disclosure. Because our data are offender-based, our information on ethnicity of offenders is more complete than our information on ethnicity of victims.

6. The Adult Criminal Court Survey (ACCS) is compiled by the Canadian Centre for Justice Statistics in Ottawa. Data in the study utilized were drawn from provincial courts in Nova Scotia, Quebec and Yukon Territory. The survey covers sexual offences from 1990 and 1991 and is strictly an offender data base.

7. Prior to 1997 many judges used the concept of a "starting point" for sentencing assaults determined to be major, having regard to the particular gravity of the conduct by duration, repetition and degree of interference with the child's bodily integrity. For major sexual assaults, the starting point was three or four years depending on the province (Ruby & Martin 1997: 291). In R.V. McDonnel (1997), the Court found that "starting points" for major sexual offences created, in effect, a new category of offences and as only parliament and not judges can create new offences, the "starting point" concept should not be used in sentencing.

8. As a result of "An Act to Amend the Criminal Code" (formerly Bill C-41), proclaimed September 3, 1996, the conditional sentencing provision was introduced. Consequently only the last year of our data set includes conditional sentences.

Chapter 6

Parental Response to Community Notification

Lisa Sutherland

Child Sexual Abuse Prevention

Beginning in the early 1980s, increased public awareness and concern about child sexual abuse resulted in the creation of numerous prevention programs, typically offered through schools and community centres. The majority of these programs, still in use today, are aimed at educating children to recognize abusive behaviour, leave the situation and disclose. In recent years, parents and professionals have begun to question the appropriateness and efficacy of a strategy that focuses solely on teaching children prevention skills. Many have begun to advocate for a shift from child-targeted prevention efforts to a more protective model that relies on educating adults to understand how offenders operate, recognize early signs of abuse and know how to deal with disclosures (Berrick & Gilbert 1991).

Community notification programs may be understood as the latest stage in the evolution of the sexual abuse prevention movement and a shift towards a community protection model. Community notification refers to the practice of providing communities with information identifying certain sexual offenders who have been released from prison, in the hopes that citizens will be able to limit the risk of future offences through increased awareness, monitoring and reduced access to vulnerable children.

Development of Community Notification Protocols

Washington was the first state to formally authorize local law enforcement to publicize information regarding high-risk offenders, beginning in 1990. Since then, federal legislation has been amended to create sex offender registration laws across the United States, with an active community notification process in all but three states (National Center for Missing and Exploited Children 1997).

Manitoba developed a similar process in February 1995, becoming the first province in Canada to approve a formal community notification protocol. Within two years, most other provinces had also developed some form of community notification.

The Manitoba Protocol is generally applied to adult offenders who have been convicted of a sexual offence, incarcerated and assessed as presenting a high risk to reoffend at the time of their release into the community. The primary objective is to "enhance public protection, through the release of appropriate information either to the public generally, or to individuals/groups within a community, when a high-risk sexual offender is or will be residing in the community " (Cooper 1995: 2). Offender information is carefully reviewed by a Community Notification Advisory Committee (CNAC) established by the Manitoba Department of Justice. CNAC members consider a range of possible responses, taking into account the risk of public alarm, the impact on past victims and the privacy rights of the offender, in making a decision regarding formal public disclosure. The Committee makes recommendations to the appropriate police agency about whether or not, and to what extent, offender information should be made public. Typically, notifications will include a picture and description of the perpetrator, a description of his (all the notification subjects to date have been male) current sexual offence(s), details of his criminal history and information regarding sentencing, treatment and substance use. Those receiving the notification are expected to assess the risk to themselves or family members and to take any action necessary to ensure their safety, with the exception of any vigilante behaviour.

CNAC considers three categories of offenders: sexual aggressors who target adult victims, incest offenders who assault blood relatives, and pedophiles who victimize children and/or adolescents. Providing parents with identifying information about a released offender theoretically presents them with the opportunity to inform their children of the potential danger, teach them sexual abuse prevention strategies and reduce the offender's access to children by monitoring his behaviour (Freeman-Longo 1996). However, it cannot be declared with any certainty that parents will act in the anticipated positive, protective ways assumed by the Manitoba Protocol.

Debating the Value of Notification

The John Howard Society of Alberta (1996) suggests that releasing offender information to the general public does nothing to enhance public safety in the absence of appropriate advice on how to interpret and act on the information provided. It is possible that citizens may respond in ways that are ineffective, harmful or even criminal.

Despite the constant possibility that unknown sexual offenders are already living in the community, the notification may create an increased and unrealistic sense of danger. Parents could become hypervigilant, needlessly reducing their child(ren)'s freedom and involvement in community activities. Community fear and anger might be directed at the identified offender in the form of protests, threats and violence, in an effort to remove him from the neighbourhood.

In their review of state and federal sex offender legislation, Matson and Lieb (1997) discuss data collected by several states that have tracked incidents of harassment towards identified sex offenders. In New Jersey, law enforcement officials received four reports of threats out of 135 notifications. This included one incident involving a physical attack on an innocent person mistaken for the identified sex offender. In Oregon, 10 percent of the offenders subject to notification reported experiencing name-calling, vandalism, threats of arson and an incident where an offender was threatened at gunpoint. Officials from Washington State reported that 3.5 percent of identified offenders experienced harassment. Half of these incidents were directed at family members of the identified offender and, in one case, the offender's intended home was burned down following the release of his identity.

Less visible reactions might include a refusal to provide housing, employment or other basic needs to the offender. If the notified community is successful in their attempts to eject the offender from their neighbourhood, he may simply move elsewhere, possibly increasing the risk to others who are not aware of his offending history.

Certainly it appears that being the subject of a notification does not discourage the offender from reoffending. The Washington State Institute for Public Policy compared the estimated reoffence rates of high-risk sex offenders subject to notification legislation with equally high-risk offenders released before the laws were implemented. They found no statistically significant difference in the recidivism rate between the two groups, suggesting that being the subject of a notification does not have an impact on offender behaviour (Schram & Milloy 1995).

An alternative concern regarding notification is the creation of a false sense of security, where community members are misled by the idea that all dangerous sexual offenders living in the community have been identified. Parents may not feel that it is necessary to do anything beyond avoiding the one person described in the media release. The notification may perpetuate the notion of a dangerous stranger rather than reminding parents that most sex offenders are people known and trusted by their victims.

Specific systems of community notification are often established because of public reaction to highly publicized cases, such as a rape-murder case, rather than because of empirical evidence that these policies actually decrease the risk of victimization (Freeman-Longo 1996). The establishment of the Manitoba Protocol was announced following the murder of teenager Sarah Kelly in The Pas, Manitoba, by a sex offender previously known only to local justice personnel, who were forbidden to warn the public of his potential risk to the community. CNAC reviewed its first case in June 1995, four months after the murder, without a complete understanding of the potential impact of the process and with no evaluative component (Collerman 1996).

It is necessary to better understand the experiences of parents who are notified of the presence of a high-risk pedophile in order to anticipate the actual versus the assumed ways that parents will interpret and use this information. In an effort to explore and describe these responses, parents of school-aged children living in a rural Manitoba city were invited to participate in a 1998 study to observe the impact of receiving a simulated notification. This chapter will describe the results of the Manitoba study, identify areas for future research and discuss policy implications.

Manitoba Parental Response Study

A series of focus groups were conducted with parents of elementary and junior high school-aged children to discuss their thoughts, feelings and anticipated behaviours in response to a simulated notification experience. A group format, rather than individual interviews, was considered most appropriate to capture both the social and personal factors influencing response. It was expected that parental interpretation and reaction to being notified would be influenced not only by their own knowledge and experiences, but also by how they saw or heard of other parents responding, by how they imagined others might respond and by how they thought others expected them to respond. Krueger (1988) suggests that an individual, answering the same questions as those discussed in a focus group, would likely provide answers quite quickly, but the group process "sparks new ideas" and reminds people of other points of view.

Focus Groups

All parents of children attending the seven elementary and junior high schools in Portage la Prairie, Manitoba, were invited by letter to participate. Interested parents were provided with the information necessary for their informed consent. Those who wished to participate received a written description of the research topic prior to attending a focus group as a way of sensitizing them to the issues to be discussed.

Although all parents have a stake in preventing child sexual abuse, it was correctly anticipated that the main interest would come from mothers (Berrick 1988). Indeed, all but one participant was female. The only father to attend came unexpectedly with his wife to the third group. His presence provided an interesting opportunity to compare his response to the notification with the responses of female participants. It also allowed observations of how he and his wife discussed the issue and negotiated a protective childcare response that they both supported. I do not consider this lone father to represent the "male perspective" on the subject and, as it was not a specific goal of this research to examine the relationship between a parent's gender and her/his response, no special effort was made to recruit more fathers for this study.

Four, two-hour focus groups were conducted, with a total of twenty-two participants. Participants had one to three school-aged children ranging in age from four to fourteen, with an almost equal number of sons and daughters among all group members. Most of the participants had one child, nine had two children and two participants had three children.

It was my impression that the level of child sexual abuse awareness amongst participants was higher than would be found in a truly random sample of parents from the community at large. Almost one third of participants had some specialized knowledge of child sexual offenders as a result of education or employment experiences. Group members included child welfare workers, school staff, a police officer, foster parents, a victim services volunteer and a women's shelter counsellor. These individuals identified having a personal and professional interest in the subject that resulted in their participation. Participants were not asked to reveal any personal knowledge or experience of childhood sexual abuse, although several members referred to their own victimization, or that of a loved one, during the discussions.

Prior to each discussion group, members completed a brief, anonymous, pre-notification questionnaire about their opinions regarding community notification. Parents were asked, for example, if they felt the police should notify the public about high-risk sex offenders and if they believed the offender's presence in the community increased their child's risk of being sexually abused. Each participant was then provided with a copy of an actual Community Notification Media Release and asked to complete four open-ended statements: "I feel ..."; "This means ..."; "When I read this I wondered ..."; and "Now that I know this, I will ...". Both questionnaires were collected and contributed to data analysis.

Every focus group discussion began with the facilitator asking participants to describe the experience of being notified. Although an interview guide was developed to ensure that specific areas of interest were included in each group's discussion, the agenda of the groups remained flexible so that participants were able to consider a variety of related topics and determine the issues most relevant to them.

Parents' Perspectives

Parents clearly want to be notified: 90 percent of participants indicated on their questionnaire that they would want to be told of the offender's presence in their neighbourhood. The provision of accurate, factual information was seen as a great improvement over the possibility of being completely unaware or relying on a community rumour. As one member observed, "If they sent this out with a picture of the guy saying he has a criminal record, I don't see how anybody could say that it's just gossip."

Participants supported the idea of community notification for all of the same reasons identified by pro-notification advocates (John Howard Society of Alberta 1996). Parents felt they had a right and a need to know, primarily because of their expectation that the identified offender would re-offend following his release. This expectation, combined with the perception that there is a lack of community resources and supervision, no effective sex offender treatment and devastation to potential victims all resulted in parents' desire for notification information.

Participants also felt that child sex offenders are worse than other criminals because they are sneaky, unpredictable and manipulative, their crimes are predatory and because of the unique vulnerability of child victims. In one group, members described a number of specific factors that contributed to this impression:

> ... their victims are helpless, they're young.... I think people see sex offenders as more likely to re-offend than others.
> Yeah, other criminals are more able to be rehabilitated.
> And how do you know how many times he offended before he got caught?
> I think we think of sexual offending as being more ingrained—it's part of that person's makeup ... and especially because the media does make a big point of just how negative it is.
> And even among other offenders, they tend to be the ones who are most often attacked.
> They even have to be segregated within the prison system.

Participants recognized the potential for the offender to experience a negative or even violent reception in the community as a result of the notification. However, they considered these consequences an appropriate punishment for his crimes and felt they were minor compared to what his victims had endured. The common sentiment was, "He made his bed, he can lie in it."

Impact of Notification

When discussing the presence of the offender in the community, the majority of parents described feeling uncertain, afraid and powerless. Several members even described feeling physically ill in response to the notification. One participant said, "I was okay until I read pedophile.... I got a sickening feeling in the pit of my stomach ... cold sweats like someone hit me."

The notification warned them of a "new" danger in the neighbourhood, even though all participants acknowledged that unidentified offenders were most likely already living among them. It also raised concerns about unidentified offenders as parents commented on the fact that "anyone" could potentially be a sex offender. As one parent noted, "a certain percentage of your population is pedophiles, so it's there already. But just having this information suddenly makes us more aware." Another shared this opinion, wondering "how many [offenders] are walking around on the streets as we speak and nobody's doing anything? ... But because they knew that someone was there [from a notification] they got frightened."

Why does being notified about one specific offender cause parents to feel that their neighbourhood has suddenly become a more dangerous environment? The notification appears to focus attention away from a general awareness of the issue to the distinct possibility that child sexual abuse might occur in their community. However, it did not appear that any participants were misled by a false sense of security into believing all sex offenders had been identified.

Along with feelings of fear, parents were more likely to express anger against, and frustration with, a justice system that, in their perception, did not keep a high-risk offender "locked up" until he was no longer such a danger to the community. As one mother stated, "If he's ever going to offend again they shouldn't let him out." Another wondered "what they classify as a high risk, and if he's high risk, why was he given the freedom?" Another said, "I would like to know why he was released because of the words 'however he is still a predator.' Why was he released?"

This was a primary theme raised early in all discussion groups—why are high-risk offenders released? The contradiction between these two pieces of information presented a major challenge to parents in their effort to understand the meaning of the notification. Participants realized that the offender was being released "because he served his full time" but they felt sentences were often too short and believed high-risk offenders should remain in jail until their threat to the community was reduced.

The language used in the notification also contributed to its impact in very powerful ways. Many of the words shocked or frightened participants. One group member said, "the word 'predator' really scares the dickens out of me." Another stated it was the details of the offence, "forcible confinement and three counts of sex abuse—that frightened me." Other words were considered too clinical or technical. While the use of Criminal Code terms lent some legitimacy to the notification, parents were left wondering what the offender had actually done to his victims. The following exchange was typical:

> I may be stupid, but what does three counts of sexual interference mean?
> That's just a nice way of saying sexual assault.
> It's just totally like assault?
> Well no, that means sometimes fondling and ...
> It can mean anything.
> It can mean them doing things to you, it can be anything sexual.

Participants argued that a better understanding of exactly how this man had offended would be valuable information in developing an appropriate child protection strategy. As one parent explained, "Terms like sexual interference make me angry because I think they're just being politically correct! If he raped someone, if he sodomized someone, let us know so that maybe it would help us with more information for our children."

Finally, the mere fact that the community was being notified about this specific offender suggested to parents that somehow he is more dangerous than other criminals and even other sexual offenders. The notification "gives the impression that somehow this is a more serious or worse or a more dangerous offender." One mother observed that "every time someone is released from prison, they don't send out a form and say this guy murdered so-and-so, but we get these on this type of criminal. So obviously this is different."

Parents agreed that although there was an initial impact, subsequent notifications would have less shock value and there might be less of a response. One member admitted, "I don't know myself if I'd pay as close attention to this as I did to the first one."

Response to Notification

Almost all participants described some aspect of their child protection strategy within seconds of reading the notification. There was a sense of obligation to take measures to protect children from the offender, even when parents were not sure what they could or should do. Parents stated that they would have to do "something" or it would feel like they were ignoring the warning. As one member put it, "I'm somehow even more responsible as a parent because I have been given this information."

One of the first things many participants thought they would do is contact family members, friends, neighbours, school personnel, police and/or agencies who were considered knowledgeable about child protection in an effort to acquire support, information and instruction. Others felt it was adequate to simply maintain their ongoing child protection practices, while a few thought it was acceptable to confront the identified offender and even pressure him to leave the community. Some participants described responding to the notification as a professional versus a parent, as an adult versus a child or as a protector versus a survivor. One mother, who identified herself as a victim of childhood sexual abuse, said she had conflicting feelings about how to respond: "the intellectual in me is agreeing with you, the child in me is saying the son-of-a-bitch should be ... you know. I'm fighting with myself inside."

Some members wondered if the offender had gained access to his victims by establishing a trust relationship with a vulnerable family, saying this indicated that not all children in the community would be at risk and this would influence the type of protection strategies they considered. Others described feeling a sense of panic, knowing the offender was "out there" and wondering if he would begin "snatching children off the playground."

Several parents worried about being overly assertive in their protection strategies for fear of triggering the offender's violence, "setting him off" or attracting his attention and becoming targeted as a victim. One participant suggested approaching the identified offender with a list of conditions for him to follow in the community. Another member expressed concern, noting that the offender was described as "potentially violent," and she wondered if trying to enforce the community conditions would "send him off on a rampage." This fear of somehow enraging the offender or triggering his offending behaviour also arose in another group. One mother said she would be reluctant to demonstrate any overtly negative reaction to the offender for fear he would "get bent out of shape or things would escalate–like maybe then he'd target my children."

Several mothers who shared parenting duties believed their own response to being notified would be calmer than their male partner's reactions. However, although the one male participant described a more confrontational approach than that of the other women in his focus group, it was similar to the responses of female members of other groups. There was nothing unique about his response in this particular study that could be attributed to gender. Many female participants indicated that, when it came to the safety of their children, they had no reservations about confronting and challenging the identified offender.

Female members of all groups referred to child protection responsibilities as their job, "not the school or the babysitter or my mother." One participant suggested this was because of the "motherly instinct that puts moms in that protective mode ... when it has to do with our children." Female group members also felt they identified more with potential victims because they themselves felt more vulnerable as women in our society.

Regardless of how they thought they might respond, parents clearly indicated they would blame themselves if they were unable to protect their own child(ren) from the offender.

Informing Children of the Danger

While the notification identified a particular offender, there was some parental uncertainty about whether their children should be informed about the notification or the risk of sexual abuse in general. Every group discussed the benefits and drawbacks of sharing the media release with a child and showing her/him the offender's picture. Participants were not sure it was a good idea to "put a face" to the offender for fear of frightening their children, while others wanted them to have some idea of what he looked like. One group member stated very definitely, "I would never show my child a picture like this and tell them to watch out for this man.... These are things that I think parents need to do to protect their kids, or be aware of."

Ironically, some of the identifying information provided in the notification, such as location and appearance, was considered to be of little use to parents as these characteristics could be easily changed. More permanent features, such as height, approximate weight, scars and tattoos were considered slightly more helpful but most parents did not believe they would remember the information long enough to make a positive identification.

In an effort to resolve their anxiety, parents in every group had numerous, but somewhat extreme, ideas for improving methods of offender identification. Forcing the offender to wear an alarm, an exploding ink bracelet or a flashing fluorescent neckband, marking him with a tattoo, branding him and spray painting his head gold were just some of the ideas discussed. Parents speculated that knowing how the identified offender operated, rather than what he looked like, would provide more useful information for identifying and avoiding high-risk situations:

> I'd like to know what's his usual pattern of enticing children.
> That's another thing you could warn your children about. If a
> man comes up to you and says this or offers you this, or does

he reach out and grab them from behind the bush, what is his usual pattern?

Prevention Education

In general, participants described the notification as a "good reminder to review street-proofing strategies with the children" and felt it promoted "active parenting." Another participant stated, "As sickening and as horrible as this is, it has jolted me to realize that I have done some street-proofing with my kids, I haven't done enough and I've got to do more." However, while the notification clearly communicates that there is a potential threat to the safety of self and / or family, it does not provide support or suggestions for how to evaluate or respond to this threat.

Most participants demonstrated a good basic knowledge of child sexual abuse. Participants were aware that most offenders are people known to their victims, often being a friend or family member, not "a dirty old man" in a trench coat. Group members were able to describe some of the indicators of abuse, thought that most abuse is never reported and believed offences were never, ever the victim's fault. Many had already discussed the issue of child sexual abuse with their children using the "know-go-tell" strategy, promoted in many formal prevention programs, that teaches children how to identify abusive behaviour, escape and disclose. The specific content of parents' prevention messages differed depending on parental knowledge, the age and gender of their children and the degree of graphic detail parents were comfortable in sharing. Those who had already discussed sexual abuse prevention with their children were far more comfortable with repeating it than parents who had not. Regardless of previous experience dealing with this topic, the most common concern expressed by all participants was how to educate children adequately without scaring them.

Although none of the participants openly admitted to having any discomfort with the topic themselves, they did wonder how parents who were uncomfortable or lacking in knowledge would educate their children on these matters. Unlike the little attention they felt parents typically paid to readily available information regarding child sexual abuse prevention, participants predicted "you send this (notification) with those guidelines and you can bet they will get read, and read thoroughly!" Another group member agreed, "It would certainly be a completely different level of interest."

Group members also suggested that a telephone help-line or a community meeting held at the time a notification was released would be helpful, "so you don't get a bunch of vigilante parents out on the loose ... or scared and misinformed kids." One member described why she thought such a meeting would be useful:

> to calm everybody—because I can just imagine some people absolutely flipping. Somebody has to be there to quell some of the fears and direct them and get them headed in the proper direction. What I'm saying is "You don't have to panic about this—we're here, and you may want to take these precautions ... what to do when you run into him, if you run into him," without setting off a real panic.

Even those who were knowledgeable and comfortable educating their children wondered how much information children were able to understand and retain as a result of prevention education efforts. Others wondered how effective any child strategy would be if a youngster was faced with an older, larger, aggressive, determined sex offender. One mother said "I don't care how prepared (children) are, if you get grabbed by someone twice your size you generally don't get away." All parents agreed that over time, their protective response would likely taper off, especially if there was no contact with, or further attention paid to, the offender.

Ultimately, parents admitted to taking a best-guess approach to prevention and just hoped their child was never approached by any offender. As one mother said, "You can tell and tell and tell them things, but you've just got to hope it just doesn't ever happen. You've just got to pray it never happens."

Monitoring the Offender and Reducing Access to Children

Although unsure of exactly what could be done to reduce the risk of victimization, parents were far more willing to accept the role of child protector than the responsibility for monitoring the offender. Participants recognized the limited ability of police and / or probation officers to keep tabs on offenders, but felt ill-equipped to carry out this task themselves. Members of one group commented, "You kind of share responsibility in watching for this guy," " But again, it's not telling you what to watch for."

Some parents wondered what they were supposed to do if they encountered the offender on the street, while others worried about what they might do if they saw him. Certain acts against the identified offender were considered unacceptable because they were against the law, but parents did not always agree on what would constitute vigilantism. Some thought it would be acceptable to confront him and advise him he was being watched, while others advocated picketing his house or running him out of town. Most participants described having vengeful thoughts but said they would never actually carry them out. A few worried they might do something "crazy" if faced with the actual offender, particularly if their own child had been victimized. Every group engaged in the following type of conversation, usually characterized by both laughter and shared silences:

> I wouldn't go out looking for this guy and wanting to hang him up by his balls from a tree.
> That might come to mind but I wouldn't actually do it.
> I'm thinking baling wire....
> ... a little elastic band...
> ... some fishing line! (laughter)
> Don't think it could never happen to you—don't say you would never ever act on those—when it happens, emotions take over your normal person and you aren't rational any more.

One participant was more concerned about not being seen by the offender, in the hopes that she could avoid being targeted, "It's almost like you'd want to hide. I'd almost want to be invisible so that maybe if he doesn't know me ... he'll leave us alone."

A lack of offender knowledge, supervisory skills, authority and resources all contributed to parents' desire that formal controls, such as paid supervisors, be provided to reduce the offender's access to children in the community. They suggested that rules be established to determine where the offender could live and work and with whom he could associate. Others thought that a halfway house or segregated community would be helpful. Opposition to offender reintegration ranged from subtle limitations on community involvement to outright hostility. Several members of one group revealed this difference of opinion in their discussion:

> I don't think I'd deny him a chance to get back into the community.....
> Ya, like I wouldn't care if he worked with me, but I wouldn't want to talk with him.
> No, I couldn't handle even being in the same room with him.
> No, I'd want to spit on him. Even the thought of it makes me very angry.

Parents were not prepared to give the offender any assistance if it meant placing other children at risk. Any difficulty finding a job, a place to live or establishing social contacts was an appropriate consequence for his having offended.

Implications of Parents' Responses to Notification

This study examined the initial impact and anticipated response of a limited number of self-selected participants, predominantly mothers, to a simulated notification experience. Although the findings reveal common themes within and across the various focus groups, they may only be cautiously generalized to similar groups and are not considered representative of the general population.

Participants clearly want to be notified if a high-risk sex offender is or will be residing in their neighbourhood. However, it appears that simply identifying the offender, without providing information on how to respond, is not enough to ensure or promote effective protective behaviour from citizens. Despite a desire to do whatever is necessary to keep their child(ren) safe, parents were forced to rely on their own knowledge of child sexual abuse prevention, and none of them were confident that what they knew was enough. Even parents with specialized sexual abuse education and professional experience were unsure of what to do.

This resulted in parents feeling uncertain, afraid and powerless. The notification was interpreted as a warning, informing them of a threat, without helping them determine what to do next. All participants wanted reassurance, support, information and direction, as evidenced by their decision to contact others to seek clarity and guidance after being notified.

Not knowing how to protect their children and live safely in the presence of the offender, the participants focused much of the discussion on ways of isolating and eliminating him from the community. Participants agreed that the ideal solution, although admittedly unrealistic, was to keep the offender in jail until he was no longer a threat or release him to a segregated community where his access to children was prohibited. When considering the physical presence of the offender in their own neighbourhood, participants promoted the idea of a paid support person, someone whom parents considered to be more capable than they were, to monitor the offender and reduce his contact with children. Parents questioned their own ability to recognize and respond to the offender effectively and wished there was some dramatic, highly visible way of identifying him to aid them in avoiding him altogether.

Justice and child protection officials must recognize and anticipate the anxiety and uncertainty experienced by parents who receive a notification. Participants identified several ways their anxiety might be reduced. It was strongly suggested that the language used in a notification be more easily understood and provide information that would be more useful to parents in planning prevention strategies. In addition to a physical description of the offender, participants suggested that notifications include information about how the offender gained access to his victim(s), his relationship to victims (if applicable), as well as a clear description of his offence(s).

Parents indicated they would welcome some specific instruction on how to respond to the notification and thought that some child protection strategies should be provided along with the notification. This could be provided as additional written information, at a community meeting or through an information "helpline." Releasing a notification also creates a valuable opportunity to provide the public with broader abuse prevention education, including information about sex-offender behaviour, indicators of abuse, what to do if one suspects a child is being abused, how to respond to disclosures and information on available community resources. This would be more consistent with the community protection model of abuse prevention being promoted by many parents and professionals who are concerned about the appropriateness of child-focused prevention efforts.

Although all participants acknowledged, in theory, the presence of unidentified offenders in their community, the notification clearly focused the majority of their attention on the identified offender. All parents were able to describe or relate to extreme and punitive protective behaviours aimed at isolating or eliminating the offender from the community. Data collected in several states demonstrate that violence and threats are not only directed at the offender but can also extend to include his family members. Ironically, these barriers to community reintegration may actually increase the dynamic risk factors that can trigger a relapse (Collerman 1996), because when the offender experiences stress, his risk of reoffending is increased. Public expressions of anger and rejection towards the offender simply "confirms his perception of adults as hostile and punitive and reinforces his attraction to children" (Groth, Hobson & Gary 1982: 131).

While it is difficult to imagine people actively welcoming a convicted sex offender into their neighbourhood(s), it makes sense to do so, based on the belief that providing the offender with emotional and practical supports can reduce the risk of reoffending. There are many opportunities for justice personnel, child protection agencies and citizens to work together in an effort to create an environment that encourages successful, safe community reintegration. An example of this is the Circles of Support and Accountability (Circles) program, a national reintegration project that operates in cooperation with Corrections Services Canada, Chaplaincy Division. The offender agrees to accept volunteer assistance, engage in recommended treatment and be accountable for acting responsibly in the community. Specially trained volunteers agree to provide emotional support and practical assistance, such as securing housing, employment, social assistance and/or helping the offender to learn to manage his leisure time. Research on the effectiveness of this approach would further our understanding of the relationship between a sex offender's reintegration into the community and the risk of reoffending.

Actively accepting the identified offender as a member of the community is likely a significant challenge for most parents. However, it is naïve to continue thinking of offenders as dangerous strangers. At the very least, notifications need to remind the community that not all offenders have been identified and that most offenders are known to their victim, gaining access by abusing positions of authority and trust. The notification process should take advantage of the opportunity to promote general abuse prevention rather than inadvertently contributing to a community response aimed at an individual offender.

Future Research

Although this study contributes to what is known about how parents may determine and initiate a response to being notified, it may be more accurate to consider parental response as a process that develops and changes over time rather than as a single decision made upon receiving the notification. It also raises many important questions and identifies areas for further research. Most obvious is a need to know more about sex offenders in order to develop the understanding necessary for early identification and intervention for individuals developing offending behaviours. Increased awareness of how sex offenders operate would also aid child protection workers and parents in using the most effective techniques for preventing offences.

Future research could examine the impact of specific variables, such as parents' age, gender, education and personal experiences, on their interpretation and responses to notification. This information might assist police and community agencies with the development of notifications and educational information that is most appropriate for particular target populations. Other factors to consider might include age and gender of children, the size and cohesiveness of the community and the ways in which the notification is released. Other methodologies, such as direct observations or interviews with several family members regarding what was actually done in response to a notification, would overcome the difficulty of relying on self-report data from a single perspective.

Conclusion

Because the notification targets a single offender whom citizens do not consider to be a member of their community, there is a serious and significant danger of reinforcing the idea of "stranger danger." The individual described by the notification, rather than his sex-offending behaviours, is presented as a danger to the community. Individualizing the threat ensures that little attention is paid to possible broader social forces or factors that might be successfully addressed in the hopes of reducing the offending behaviours. It also fails to remind parents that there are many unidentified offenders, people who are most often known and trusted members of the community, who may pose a far greater risk to their children than the identified offender.

It appears that the most effective implementation of a community notification would include the provision of community education and support. This would require increased collaboration and information sharing between social service providers, justice personnel and citizens. Community members could not only be educated but involved and empowered in the effort to reduce the risk of reoffence in ways that more comfortably address their dual roles of child protector and offender monitor, as with the Circles of Support and Accountability project.

This study demonstrates that parents currently attempt to respond in ways that are consistent with the expectations of pro-notification advocates. That is, they acknowledge the risk of abuse and engage in child protection strategies. However, without providing some support and education aimed at increasing parental knowledge and confidence, those receiving notification may well continue to feel anxious and incompetent rather than empowered to do what they feel is expected of them as parents and community members.

References

Achenbach, T.M. 1991. *Manual for the Child Behavior Checklist/4-18 and 1991 Profile*. Burlington, VT: University Associates in Psychiatry.

Ackerman, N.W. 1966. *Treating the Troubled Family*. New York: Basic Books.

Adams-Tucker, C., and P.L. Adams. 1984. "Treatment of Sexually Abused Children." In I.R. Stuart and J.G. Greer (eds.), *Victims of Sexual Aggression: Treatment of Children, Women, and Men*. New York: Van Nostrand Reinhold.

Alter-Reid, K., M.S. Gibbs, J.R. Lachenmeyer, J. Sigal and N.A. Massoth. 1986. "Sexual Abuse of Children: A Review of the Empirical Findings." *Clinical Psychology Review* 6.

Anderson, C., and P. Mayes. 1982. "Treating Family Sexual Abuse: The Humanistic Approach." *Journal of Child Care* 1.

Badgley, R. 1984. *Sexual Offences Against Children: Report of the Committee on Sexual Offences Against Children and Youth, Volume 1*. Ottawa: Supply and Services Canada.

Bagley, C. 1985. "Child Sexual Abuse: A Child Welfare Perspective." In K.L. Levitt and B. Wharf (eds.), *The Challenge of Child Welfare*. Vancouver: University of British Columbia Press.

_____. 1988. *Child Sexual Abuse in Canada: Further Analysis of the 1983 National Survey*. Ottawa: National Health and Welfare.

_____. 1991a. "The Prevalence and Mental Health Sequels of Child Sexual Abuse in a Community Sample of Women Aged 18 to 27." *Canadian Journal of Community Mental Health* 10.

_____. 1991b. "Preventing Child Sexual Abuse: The State of Knowledge and Future Research." In C. Bagley and R. Thomlinson (eds.), *Child Sexual Abuse: Critical Perspectives on Prevention, Intervention, and Treatment*. Toronto: Wall & Emerson.

Bagley, C., and K. King. 1990. *Child Sexual Abuse: The Search For Healing*. New York: Tavistock/Routledge.

Bagley, C., and R. Ramsay. 1986. "Sexual Abuse in Childhood: Psychosocial Outcomes and Implications for Social Work Practice." *Journal of Social Work and Human Sexuality* 4.

Bagley, C., M. Wood and L. Young. 1994. "Victim to Abuser: Mental Health and Behavioral Sequels of Child Sexual Abuse in a Community Survey of Young Adult Males." *Child Abuse and Neglect* 18.

Bagley, C., and L. Young. 1988. "Depression, Self-Esteem and Suicidal Behaviour as Sequels of Sexual Abuse in Childhood: Research and Therapy." In

G. Cameron (ed.), *Child Maltreatment: Expanded Concepts of Helping*. New York: Lawrence Erlbaum.

Baker, A.W., and S.P. Duncan. 1985. "Child Sexual Abuse: A Study of Prevalence in Great Britain." *Child Abuse and Neglect* 9.

Barbarin, O.A., and M. Chesler. 1986. "The Medical Context of Parental Coping with Childhood Cancer." *American Journal of Community Psychology* 14.

Barnett, O.W., C.L. Miller-Perrin and R.D. Perrin. 1997. *Family Violence Across the Lifespan: An Introduction*. Thousand Oaks, CA: Sage.

Becker, J.V. 1994. "Offender: Characteristics and Treatment." *The Future of Children: Sexual Abuse of Children* 4(2).

Becker, J.V., and B. Bonner. 1998. "Sexual and Other Abuse of Children." In R.J. Morris and T.R. Kratochwill (eds.), *The Practice of Child Therapy*. Third edition. Boston: Allyn & Bacon.

Beitchman, J.H., K.J. Zucker, J.E. Hood, G.A. DaCosta and D. Akman. 1991. "A Review of the Short-Term Effects of Child Sexual Abuse." *Child Abuse and Neglect* 15.

Beitchman, J.H., K.J. Zucker, J.E. Hood, G.A. daCosta, D. Akman and E. Cassavia. 1992. "A Review of the Long-Term Effects of Child Sexual Abuse." *Child Abuse and Neglect* 16.

Bentovim, A., and H. Ratner. 1991. "Sibling Abuse in a Reconstituted Family: A Focal Family Therapy Approach." In W.N. Friedrich (ed.), *Casebook of Sexual Abuse Treatment*. New York: W.W. Norton and Company.

Berliner, L. 1997. "Trauma-Specific Therapy for Sexually Abused Children." In D.A. Wolfe, R.J. McMahon and R.D. Peters (eds.), *Child Abuse: New Directions in Prevention and Treatment Across the Lifespan*. Thousand Oaks, CA: Sage Publications.

Berliner, L., and D.M. Elliott. 1996. "Sexual Abuse of Children." In J. Briere et al. (eds.), *The APSAC Handbook on Child Maltreatment*. Thousand Oaks, CA: Sage Publications.

Berliner, L., and E. Ernst. 1984. "Group Work With Preadolescent Sexual Assault Victims." In I.R. Stuart and J.G. Greer (eds.), *Victims of Sexual Aggression: Treatment of Children, Women, and Men*. New York: Van Nostrand Reinhold.

Berliner, L., and J.R. Wheeler. 1987. "Treating the Effects of Sexual Abuse on Children." *Journal of Interpersonal Violence* 2.

Berman, P. 1990. "Group Therapy Techniques for Sexually Abused Preteen Girls." *Child Welfare* 69.

Berrick, J. 1988. "Parental Involvement in Child Abuse Prevention Training: What Do They Learn?" *Child Abuse and Neglect* 12.

Berrick, J., and N. Gilbert. 1991. *With the Best of Intentions: The Child Sexual Abuse Prevention Movement*. New York: Guilford Press.

Billings, A.G., and R.H. Moos. 1981. "The Role of Coping Responses and Social Resources in Attenuating the Stress of Life Events." *Journal of Behavioral Medicine* 4.

_____. 1984. "Coping, Stress, and Social Resources Among Adults with Unipolar Depression." *Journal of Personality and Social Psychology* 46.

Bisenthal, L., and J. Clement. 1992. *Canadian Statistics on Child Sexual Abuse*. Ottawa: Department of Justice Canada, Research and Statistics Directorate, TR1992-14e.

Boney-McCoy, S., and D. Finkelhor. 1995. "Prior Victimization: A Risk Factor for Child Sexual Abuse and for PTSD-Related Symptomatology among Sexually Abused Youth." *Child Abuse and Neglect* 19.

Bonner, B., L. Kaufman, C. Harbeck and M. Brassard. 1992. "Child Maltreatment." In C.E. Walker & M.C. Roberts (eds.), *Handbook of Clinical Child Psychology*. Second edition. New York: Wiley.

Briere, J.N. 1992. *Child Abuse Trauma: Theory and Treatment of the Lasting Effects.* Newbury Park, CA: Sage Publications.

Briere, J.N., and D.M. Elliott. 1994. "Immediate and Long-Term Impacts of Child Sexual Abuse." *The Future of Children: Sexual Abuse of Children* 4(2).

Briere, J., and M. Runtz. 1986. "Suicidal Thoughts and Behaviours in Former Sexual Abuse Victims." *Canadian Journal of Behavioural Science* 18.

Browne, A., and D. Finkelhor. 1986. "Impact of Child Sexual Abuse: A Review of the Research." *Psychological Bulletin* 99.

Browning, D.H., and B. Boatman. 1977. "Incest: Children at Risk." *American Journal of Psychiatry* 134.

Burford, G., and J. Pennell. 1995. "Family Group Decision Making: An Innovation in Child and Family Welfare." In J. Hudson and B. Galaway (eds.), *Child Welfare in Canada: Research and Policy Implications.* Toronto: Thompson Educational Publishing, Inc.

Cameron, C. 2000. *Resolving Childhood Trauma: A Long-Term Study of Abuse Survivors.* Thousand Oaks, CA: Sage Publications.

Campbell Research Associates. 1992a. *Review and Monitoring of Child Sexual Abuse Cases in Hamilton-Wentworth, Ontario.* Ottawa: Department of Justice.

_____. 1992b. *Program Review of the Child Victim-Witness Support Project.* Ottawa: Department of Justice.

Canadian Justice Statistics. 1994. *Statistics Canada Report: Family Violence in Canada, Current National Data.* Ottawa: Department of Justice.

Carl, D., and G.J. Jurkovic. 1983. "Agency Triangles: Problems in Agency Family Relations." *Family Process* 22.

Carlson, E.B., L. Furby, J. Armstrong and J. Shlaes. 1997. "A Conceptual Framework for the Long-Term Psychological Effects of Traumatic Childhood Abuse." *Child Maltreatment* 2(3).

Carter, B.J. 1993. "Child Sexual Abuse: Impact on Mothers." *Affilia* 8.

_____. 1999. *Who's To Blame? Child Sexual Abuse and Non-Offending Mothers.* Toronto: University of Toronto Press.

Chapman-Smyth, E. 1993. *Evaluation of the Group Treatment Component of the Sexual Abuse Treatment Program.* Winnipeg: Unpublished manuscript.

Chethik, M. 1989. *Techniques of Child Therapy: Psychodynamic Strategies.* New York: Guilford Press.

Christiansen, J.R., and R.H. Blake. 1990. "The Grooming Process in Father-Daughter Incest." In A.L. Horton et al. (eds.), *The Incest Perpetrator: A Family Member No One Wants to Treat.* Newbury Park, CA: Sage Publications.

Cohen, J.A., and A.P. Mannarino. 1993. "A Treatment Model for Sexually Abused Preschoolers." *Journal of Interpersonal Violence* 8.

_____. 1996a. "Factors That Mediate Treatment Outcome of Sexually Abused Preschool Children." *Journal of the American Academy of Child and Adolescent Psychiatry* 35.

_____. 1996b. "A Treatment Outcome Study for Sexually Abused Preschool

Children: Initial Findings." *Journal of the American Academy of Child and Adolescent Psychiatry* 35.

_____. 1997. "A Treatment Study for Sexually Abused Preschool Children: Outcome During a One-Year Follow-Up." *Journal of the American Academy of Child and Adolescent Psychiatry* 36.

_____. 1998a. "Factors That Mediate Treatment Outcome of Sexually Abused Preschool Children: Six- and 12-Month Followup." *Journal of the American Academy of Child and Adolescent Psychiatry* 37.

_____. 1998b. "Interventions for Sexually Abused Children: Initial Treatment Outcome Findings." *Child Maltreatment* 3.

Cohen, T. 1983. "The Incestuous Family Revisited." *Social Casework* 64.

Collerman, H. 1996. *Sarah Kelly Inquest Report*. Winnipeg, Manitoba: Department of Justice.

Connors, E., and M.L.B. Oates, Jr. 1997. "The Emergence of Sexual Abuse Treatment Models within First Nations Communities." In D.A. Wolfe, R.J. McMahon and R.D. Peters (eds.), *Child Abuse: New Directions in Prevention and Treatment Across the Lifespan*. Thousand Oaks, CA: Sage Publications.

Conte, J.R., and L. Berliner. 1988. "The Impact of Sexual Abuse On Children: Empirical Findings." In L.E.A. Walker (ed.), *Handbook On Sexual Abuse of Children: Assessment and Treatment Issues*. New York: Springer Publishing Company.

Conte, J.R., and J.R. Schuerman. 1987. "Factors Associated with an Increased Impact of Child Sexual Abuse." *Child Abuse and Neglect* 11.

_____. 1988. "The Effects of Sexual Abuse on Children: A Multidimensional View." In G.E. Wyatt and G.J. Powell (eds.), *Lasting Effects of Child Sexual Abuse*. Newbury Park, CA: Sage Publications.

Conte, J.R., S. Wolf and T. Smith. 1989. "What Sexual Offenders Tell Us About Prevention Strategies." *Child Abuse and Neglect* 13.

Cooper, J. 1995. *Manitoba Community Notification Advisory Committee: Report (Number 1)*. Winnipeg: Department of Justice.

Coopersmith, S. 1981. *SEI: Self-Esteem Inventories*. Palo Alto, CA: Consulting Psychologists Press.

Corcoran, J. 1998. "In Defense of Mothers of Sexual Abuse Victims." *Families in Society* 79.

Corey, G. 2001. *Theory and Practice of Counseling and Psychotherapy*. Belmont, CA: Brooks/Cole.

Correctional Service of Canada. 1996. *Profile of Aboriginal Sexual Offenders*. Ottawa: Department of Justice.

Crosson-Tower, C. 1999. *Understanding Child Abuse and Neglect*. Needham Heights, MA: Allyn and Bacon.

Deblinger, E., C.R. Hathaway, J. Lippman and R. Steer. 1993. "Psychosocial Characteristics and Correlates of Symptom Distress in Nonoffending Mothers of Sexually Abused Children." *Journal of Interpersonal Violence* 8.

Deblinger, E., and A.H. Heflin. 1996. *Treating Sexually Abused Children and their Nonoffending Parents: A Cognitive Behavioral Approach*. Thousand Oaks, CA: Sage Publications.

Deblinger, E., J. Lippmann and R.A. Steer. 1996. "Sexually Abused Children Suffering Posttraumatic Stress Symptoms: Initial Treatment Outcome Findings." *Child Maltreatment* 1.

Deblinger, E., S.V. McLeer and D. Henry. 1990. "Cognitive Behavioral Treatment for Sexually Abused Children Suffering Post-Traumatic Stress: Preliminary Findings." *Journal of the American Academy of Child and Adolescent Psychiatry* 29.

Deblinger, E., L. Stauffer and C. Landsberg. 1994. "The Impact of a History of Child Sexual Abuse on Maternal Response to Allegations of Sexual Abuse Concerning Her Child." *Journal of Child Sexual Abuse* 3.

Deblinger, E., R.A. Steer and J. Lippmann. 1999. "Two-Year Follow-Up Study of Cognitive Behavioral Therapy for Sexually Abused Children Suffering Post-Traumatic Stress Symptoms." *Child Abuse and Neglect* 23.

De Jong, A.R. 1986. "Childhood Sexual Abuse Precipitating Maternal Hospitalization." *Child Abuse and Neglect* 10.

_____. 1988. "Maternal Responses to the Sexual Abuse of their Children." *Pediatrics* 81.

De Luca, R.V., D.A. Boyes, P. Furer, A.D. Grayston and D. Hiebert-Murphy. 1992. "Group Treatment for Child Sexual Abuse." *Canadian Psychology* 33.

De Luca, R.V., D.A. Boyes, A.D. Grayston and E. Romano. 1995. "Sexual Abuse: Effects of Group Therapy on Preadolescent Girls." *Child Abuse Review* 4.

De Luca, R.V., A.D. Grayston and E. Romano. 1999. "Sexually Abused Boys." In C.E. Schaefer (ed.), *Short-Term Psychotherapy Groups for Children: Adapting Group Processes for Specific Problems*. New York: Aronson.

De Luca, R.V., A. Hazen and J. Cutler. 1993. "Evaluation of a Group Counseling Program for Preadolescent Female Victims of Incest." *Elementary School Guidance and Counseling* 28.

De Maio, R.X. 1995. "Helping Families Become Places of Healing: Systemic Treatment of Intrafamilial Sexual Abuse." In L. Combrinck-Graham (ed.), *Children in Families at Risk: Maintaining the Connections*. New York: The Guilford Press.

Dempster, H.L. 1992. *The Aftermath of Child Sexual Abuse: The Woman's Perspective*. London: HMSO.

deYoung, M. 1994. "Immediate Maternal Reactions to the Disclosure or Discovery of Incest." *Journal of Family Violence* 9.

Dietz, C.A., and J.L. Craft. 1980. "Family Dynamics of Incest: A New Perspective." *Social Casework* 61.

DiGiorgio-Miller, J. 1998. "Sibling Incest: Treatment of the Family and the Offender." *Child Welfare* 77(3).

DiPietro, S.B. 1987. "The Effects of Intrafamilial Child Sexual Abuse on the Adjustment and Attitudes of Adolescents." *Violence and Victims* 2.

Einbender, A.J., and W.N. Friedrich. 1989. "Psychological Functioning and Behavior of Sexually Abused Girls." *Journal of Consulting and Clinical Psychology* 57.

Elbow, M., and J. Mayfield. 1991. "Mothers of Incest Victims: Villains, Victims, or Protectors?" *Families in Society* 72.

Esparza, D. 1993. "Maternal Support and Stress Response in Sexually Abused Girls Ages 6–12." *Issues in Mental Health Nursing* 14.

Everson, M.D., W.N. Hunter, D.K. Runyon, G.A. Edelsohn and M.L. Coulter. 1989. "Maternal Support following Disclosure of Incest." *American Journal of Orthopsychiatry* 59.

Everstine, D.S., and L. Everstine. 1989. *Sexual Trauma in Children and Adoles-*

cents: Dynamics and Treatment. New York: Brunner/Mazel, Inc.

Faller, K.C. 1988. "The Myth of the 'Collusive Mother': Variability in the Functioning of Mothers of Victims of Intrafamilial Sexual Abuse." *Journal of Interpersonal Violence* 3.

_____. 1989. "Why Sexual Abuse? An Exploration of the Intergenerational Hypothesis." *Child Abuse and Neglect* 13(3).

_____. 1990. "Sexual Abuse by Paternal Caretakers: A Comparison of Abusers who are Biological Fathers in Intact Families, Stepfathers and Noncustodial Fathers." In A.L. Horton et al. (eds.), *The Incest Perpetrator: A Family Member No One Wants to Treat.* Newbury Park, CA: Sage Publications.

Farrell, S.P., A.A. Hains and W.H. Davies. 1998. "Cognitive Behavioral Interventions for Sexually Abused Children Exhibiting PTSD Symptomatology." *Behavior Therapy* 29.

Finkelhor, D. 1979. *Sexually Victimized Children.* New York: The Free Press.

_____. 1984. *Child Sexual Abuse: New Theory and Research.* New York: The Free Press.

_____. 1986a. "Abusers: Special Topics." In D. Finkelhor (ed.), *A Sourcebook on Child Sexual Abuse.* Newbury Park, CA: Sage Publications.

_____. 1986b. "Sexual Abuse: Beyond the Family Systems Approach." In T.S. Trepper and M.J. Barrett (eds.), *Treating Incest: A Multiple Systems Perspective.* New York: The Haworth Press.

_____. 1987. "New Myths about Child Sexual Abuse." Paper presented (in French) at the Symposium on Child Sexual Abuse in Ottawa, May, 1987. Translated and available from the National Clearinghouse on Family Violence Prevention. Ottawa: Health and Welfare Canada.

Finkelhor, D., N. Asdigian and J. Dziuba-Leatherman. 1995. "The Effectiveness of Victimization Prevention Instruction: An Evaluation of Children's Responses to Actual Threats and Assaults." *Child Abuse and Neglect* 19.

Finkelhor, D., and L. Berliner. 1995. "Research on the Treatment of Sexually Abused Children: A Review and Recommendations." *Journal of the American Academy of Child and Adolescent Psychiatry* 34.

Finkelhor, D., and A. Browne. 1985. "The Traumatic Impact of Child Sexual Abuse: A Conceptualization." *American Journal of Orthopsychiatry* 55.

Finkelhor, D., G. Hotaling, I.A. Lewis and C. Smith. 1990. "Sexual Abuse in a National Survey of Adult Men and Women: Prevalence, Characteristics and Risk Factors." *Child Abuse and Neglect* 14.

Finkelhor, D., and D. Russell, 1984. "Women as Perpetrators: Review of the Evidence." In D. Finkelhor (ed.), *Child Sexual Abuse: New Theory and Research.* New York: Free Press.

Fischer, D., and K. Tchang. 1994. *Evaluation of the Saskatchewan Family Treatment Program for Sexually Abused Children.* Ottawa: Health and Welfare Canada.

Folkman, S., and J.T. Moskowitz. 2000. "Positive Affect and the Other Side of Coping." *American Psychologist* 55.

Freeman-Longo, R. 1996. "Feel Good Legislation: Prevention or Calamity." *Child Abuse and Neglect* 20.

Friedrich, W.N. 1979. "Predictors of the Coping Behavior of Mothers of Handicapped Children." *Journal of Consulting and Clinical Psychology* 47.

_____. 1990. *Psychotherapy of Sexually Abused Children and their Families.* New York: Norton.

_____. 1991. "Mothers of Sexually Abused Children: An MMPI Study." *Journal of Clinical Psychology* 47.

_____. 1996. "Clinical Considerations of Empirical Treatment Studies of Abused Children." *Child Maltreatment* 1(4).

Friedrich, W.N., R.L. Beilke and A.J. Urquiza. 1987. "Children From Sexually Abusive Families: A Behavioral Comparison." *Journal of Interpersonal Violence* 2.

Friedrich, W.N., L. Berliner, A.J. Urquiza and R.L. Beilke. 1988. "Brief Diagnostic Group Treatment of Sexually Abused Boys." *Journal of Interpersonal Violence* 3.

Friedrich, W.N., P. Grambsch, D. Broughton, J. Kuiper and R.L. Beilke. 1991. "Normative Sexual Behavior in Children." *Pediatrics* 88.

Friedrich, W.N., W.J. Luecke, R.L. Beilke and V. Place. 1992. "Psychotherapy Outcome of Sexually Abused Boys: An Agency Study." *Journal of Interpersonal Violence* 7.

Friedrich, W.N., and R.A. Reams. 1987. "Course of Psychological Symptoms in Sexually Abused Young Children." *Psychotherapy* 24.

Friedrich, W.N., A.J. Urquiza and R.L. Beilke. 1986. "Behavior Problems in Sexually Abused Young Children." *Journal of Pediatric Psychology* 11.

Fromuth, M.E. 1986. "The Relationship of Childhood Sexual Abuse with Later Psychological and Sexual Adjustment in a Sample of College Women." *Child Abuse and Neglect* 10.

Giarretto, H. 1981. "A Comprehensive Child Sexual Abuse Treatment Program." In P. Mrazek and C.H. Kempe (eds.), *Sexually Abused Children and their Families*. New York: Pergamon Press.

Gil, E. 1991. *The Healing Power of Play: Working with Abused Children*. New York: Guilford Press.

_____. 1996. *Systemic Treatment of Families Who Abuse*. San Francisco: Jossey-Bass Publishers.

Gilgun, J.F., and T.M. Connor. 1989. "How Perpetrators View Child Sexual Abuse." *Social Work* 34.

Goodwin, J. 1981. "Suicide Attempts in Sexual Abuse Victims and their Mothers." *Child Abuse and Neglect* 5.

Goodwin, J., T. McCarthy and P. DiVasto. 1981. "Prior Incest in Mothers of Abused Children." *Child Abuse and Neglect* 5.

Gordon, L. 1955. "Incest as Revenge against the Pre-Oedipal Mother." *Psychoanalytic Review* 42.

Gordon, M. 1990. "Males and Females as Victims of Childhood Sexual Abuse: An Examination of the Gender Effect." *Journal of Family Violence* 5.

Grayston, A.D., and R.V. De Luca. 1995. "Group Therapy for Boys Who Have Experienced Sexual Abuse: Is it the Treatment of Choice?" *Journal of Child and Adolescent Group Therapy* 5 (2).

_____. 1996. "Social Validity of Group Treatment for Sexually Abused Boys." *Child and Family Behavior Therapy* 18(2).

_____. 1999. "Female Perpetrators of Child Sexual Abuse: A Review of the Clinical and Empirical Literature." *Aggression and Violent Behavior* 4.

Grayston, A.D., R.V. De Luca and D.A. Boyes. 1992. "Self-Esteem, Anxiety, and Loneliness in Preadolescent Girls Who Have Experienced Sexual Abuse." *Child Psychiatry and Human Development* 22.

Grayston, A.D., E. Romano, R.V. De Luca and M.A. Gillis. 1997. "Determinants of Treatment Outcome in Cases of Sexual Abuse." Paper presented at the Annual Convention of the Canadian Psychological Association, June, Toronto, Ontario.

Groff, M.G. 1987. "Characteristics of Incest Offenders' Wives." *Journal of Sex Research* 23.

Groth, A., W. Hobson and T. Gary. 1982. "The Child Molester: Clinical Observations." In J. Conte & D. Shore (eds.), *Social Work and Child Sexual Abuse*. New York: Haworth.

Guntheil, T.G., and N.C. Avery. 1977. "Multiple Overt Incest as Family Defense against Loss." *Family Process* 16.

Hack, T.F., T.A.G. Osachuk and R.V. De Luca. 1994. "Group Treatment for Sexually Abused Preadolescent Boys." *Families in Society: The Journal of Contemporary Human Services* 75.

Hall-Marley, S.E., and L. Damon. 1993. "Impact of Structured Group Therapy on Young Victims of Sexual Abuse." *Journal of Child and Adolescent Group Therapy* 3(1).

Haugaard, J.J., and N.D. Reppucci. 1988. *The Sexual Abuse of Children: A Comprehensive Guide to Current Knowledge and Intervention Strategies*. San Francisco: Jossey-Bass.

Hayashino, D.S., S.K. Wurtele and K.J. Klebe. 1995. "Child Molesters: An Examination of Cognitive Factors." *Journal of Interpersonal Violence* 10(1).

Herman, J.L. 1981. *Father-Daughter Incest*. Cambridge, MA: Harvard University Press.

Hiebert-Murphy, D. 1998. "Emotional Distress among Mothers Whose Children Have Been Sexually Abused: The Role of a History of Child Sexual Abuse, Social Support, and Coping." *Child Abuse and Neglect* 22.

_____. 2000a. "Factors Related to Mothers' Perceptions of Parenting following their Children's Disclosures of Sexual Abuse." *Child Maltreatment* 5.

_____. 2000b. "Partner Abuse among Mothers Whose Children Have Been Sexually Abused: An Exploratory Study." Manuscript under review.

Hiebert-Murphy, D., and L. Burnside. 2000. "Coping among Mothers of Children Who Have Been Sexually Abused." Manuscript in progress.

Hiebert-Murphy, D., R.V. De Luca and M. Runtz. 1992. "Group Treatment for Sexually Abused Girls: Evaluating Outcome." *Families in Society: The Journal of Contemporary Human Services* 73.

Holahan, C.J., and R.H. Moos. 1986. "Personality, Coping, and Family Resources in Stress Resistance: A Longitudinal Analysis." *Journal of Personality and Social Psychology* 51.

_____. 1987. "Risk, Resistance, and Psychological Distress: A Longitudinal Analysis with Adults and Children." *Journal of Abnormal Psychology* 96.

_____. 1991. "Life Stressors, Personal and Social Resources, and Depression: A 4-Year Structural Model." *Journal of Abnormal Psychology* 100.

Holmes, T.H., and R.H. Rahe. 1967. "The Social Readjustment Rating Scale." *Journal of Psychosomatic Research* 11.

Hooper, C. 1989. "Alternatives to Collusion: The Response of Mothers to Child Sexual Abuse in the Family." *Educational and Child Psychology* 6.

_____. 1992. *Mothers Surviving Child Sexual Abuse*. London: Tavistock/Routledge.

Hornick, J., and F. Bolitho. 1992. *A Review of the Implementation of the Child*

Sexual Abuse Legislation in Selected Sites. Ottawa: Department of Justice.

Hornick, J.P., B. Burrows, D. Perry and F. Bolitho 1992. *Review and Monitoring of Child Sexual Abuse Cases in Selected Sites in Alberta.* Ottawa: Department of Justice.

Imber-Black, E. 1988. *Family and Larger Systems: A Family Therapist's Guide through the Labyrinth.* New York: The Guilford Press.

Inderbitzen-Pisaruk, H., C.R. Shawchuck and T.S. Hoier. 1992. "Behavioral Characteristics of Child Victims of Sexual Abuse: A Comparison Study." *Journal of Clinical Child Psychology* 21.

Jackson, D.D. 1957. "The Question of Family Homeostasis." *Psychiatric Quarterly Supplement* 31(1).

James, B. 1989. *Treating Traumatized Children: New Insights and Creative Interventions.* Toronto: Lexington Books.

James, B., and M. Nasjleti. 1983. *Treating Sexually Abused Children and their Families.* Palo Alto, CA: Consulting Psychologists Press, Inc.

Jenkins, A. 1990. *Invitations to Responsibility: The Therapeutic Engagement of Men Who Are Violent and Abusive.* Australia: Dulwich Centre Publications.

John Howard Society of Alberta. 1996. "Community Notification." *The Reporter* 13.

Johnson, J.T. 1992. *Mothers of Incest Survivors: Another Side of the Story.* Bloomington: Indiana University Press.

Johnson, J., W. Rasbury and L. Siegel. 1986. *Approaches to Child Treatment: Introduction to Theory, Research, and Practice.* New York: Pergamon.

Joyce, P.A. 1997. "Mothers of Sexually Abused Children and the Concept of Collusion: A Literature Review." *Journal of Child Sexual Abuse* 6.

Julian, V., and C. Mohr. 1979. "Father-Daughter Incest: Profile of the Offender." *Victimology* 4.

Justice, B., and R. Justice. 1979. *The Broken Taboo: Sex in the Family.* New York: Human Sciences Press.

Kaufman, I., A.L. Peck and K. Tagiuri. 1954. "The Family Constellation and Overt Incestuous Relations between Father and Daughter." *American Journal of Orthopsychiatry* 24.

Keller, R.A., L.F. Cicchinelli and D.M. Gardner. 1989. "Characteristics of Child Sexual Abuse Treatment Programs." *Child Abuse and Neglect* 13.

Kelley, S.J. 1990. "Parental Stress Response to Sexual Abuse and Ritualistic Abuse of Children in Day-Care Centers." *Nursing Research* 39.

Kendall-Tackett, K.A., L.M. Williams and D. Finkelhor. 1993. "Impact of Sexual Abuse on Children: A Review and Synthesis of Recent Empirical Studies." *Psychological Bulletin* 113.

Kercher, G.A., and M. McShane. 1984. "The Prevalence of Child Sexual Abuse Victimization in an Adult Sample of Texas Residents." *Child Abuse and Neglect* 8.

Kessler, R.C., R.H. Price and C.B. Wortman. 1985. "Social Factors in Psychopathology: Stress, Social Support, and Coping Processes." *Annual Review of Psychology* 36.

Kitchur, M., and R. Bell. 1989. "Group Psychotherapy With Preadolescent Sexual Abuse Victims: Literature Review and Description of an Inner-City Group." *International Journal of Group Psychotherapy* 39.

Kruczek, T., and S. Vitanza. 1999. "Treatment Effects with an Adolescent Abuse

Survivor's Group." *Child Abuse and Neglect* 23.

Krueger, R. 1988. *Focus Groups: A Practical Guide for Applied Research*. Newbury Park, CA: Sage Publications.

Kweller, R.B., and S.A. Ray. 1992. "Group Treatment of Latency-Age Male Victims of Sexual Abuse." *Journal of Child Sexual Abuse* 1(4).

Lazarus, R.S. 2000. "Toward Better Research on Stress and Coping." *American Psychologist* 55.

Lazarus, R.S., and R. Launier. 1978. "Stress-Related Transactions between Person and Environment." In L.A. Pervin and M. Lewis (eds.), *Perspectives in Interactional Psychology*. New York: Plenum Press.

Lépine, D. 1990. "Ending the Cycle of Violence: Overcoming Guilt in Incest Survivors." In T.A. Laidlaw, C. Malmo et al. (eds.), *Healing Voices: Feminist Approaches to Therapy with Women*. San Francisco: Jossey-Bass Publishers.

Liberman, R.P. 1972. "Behavioral Methods in Group and Family Therapy." *Seminars in Psychiatry* 4.

Lisak, D., Hopper, J., and Song, P. 1996. "Factors in the cycle of violence: Gender rigidity and emotional constriction." *Journal of Traumatic Stress* 9.

Lustig, N., J.W. Dresser, S.W. Spellman and T.B. Murray. 1966. "Incest: A Family Group Survival Pattern." *Archives of General Psychiatry* 14.

Lyons, J.A. 1987. "Posttraumatic Stress Disorder in Children and Adolescents: A Review of the Literature." *Developmental and Behavioral Pediatrics* 8.

MacDonald, G., K. Levine, E. Adkins, B. Trute, D. Shannon, and D. deLucia. 1996. "Avoiding Agency Triangles in Child Sexual Abuse Work: Lessons from the Manitoba Rural Child Sexual Abuse Project." Winnipeg: Unpublished manuscript.

MacKinnon, L.K. 1998. *Trust and Betrayal in the Treatment of Child Abuse*. New York: Guilford Press.

MacMillan, H.L., J.H. MacMillan, D.R. Offord, L. Griffith and A. MacMillan. 1994. "Primary Prevention of Child Sexual Abuse: A Critical Review: Part II." *Journal of Child Psychology and Psychiatry and Allied Disciplines* 35.

Maddock, J.W., and N.R. Larson. 1995. *Incestuous Families: An Ecological Approach to Understanding and Treatment*. New York: W.W. Norton and Company.

Malamuth, N.M. 1981. "Rape Fantasies as a Function of Exposure to Violent-Sexual Stimuli." *Archives of Sexual Behavior* 10.

Manion, I.G., J. McIntyre, P. Firestone, M. Ligezinska, R. Ensom and G. Wells. 1996. "Secondary Traumatization in Parents Following the Disclosure of Extrafamilial Child Sexual Abuse: Initial Effects." *Child Abuse and Neglect* 11.

Mannarino, A.P., and J.A. Cohen. 1986. "A Clinical-Demographic Study of Sexually Abused Children." *Child Abuse and Neglect* 10.

Marshall, W.L., and L.E. Marshall. 2000. "The Origins of Sexual Offending." *Trauma, Violence, and Abuse* 1(3).

Marvasti, J.A. 1994. "Play Diagnosis and Play Therapy with Child Victims of Incest." In K.J. O'Connor and C.E. Schaefer (eds.), *Handbook of Play Therapy: Volume 2: Advances and Innovations*. New York: Wiley.

Masson, J.M. 1984. *The Assault on Truth*. New York: Farrar, Straus, and Giroux.

Matson, S., and R. Lieb. 1997. *Megan's Law: A Review of State and Federal Legislation*. Seattle, WA: Washington Institute for Public Policy.

McEvoy, M., and J. Daniluk. 1995. "Wounds to the Soul: The Experiences of Aboriginal Women as Survivors of Sexual Abuse." *Canadian Psychology* 36.

McIntyre, K. 1981. "Role of Mothers in Father-Daughter Incest: A Feminist Analysis." *Social Work* 26.

McLeer, S.V., E. Deblinger, M. Atkins, E. Foa and D. Ralphe. 1988. "Posttraumatic Stress Disorder in Sexually Abused Children: A Prospective Study." *Journal of the American Academy of Child and Adolescent Psychiatry* 27.

Mednick, M. 1987. "Single Mothers: A Review and Critique of Current Research." *Applied Social Psychology Annual* 7.

Melnechuk, C. 1988. *The Integrated Treatment Model (ITM) For Sexually Abused Children and their Mothers: Final Report.* Vancouver: Vancouver Incest and Sexual Abuse Centre of Family Services of Greater Vancouver.

Merrick, M.V., B.M. Allen, and S.J. Crase. 1994. "Variables Associated with Positive Treatment Outcomes for Children Surviving Sexual Abuse." *Journal of Child Sexual Abuse* 3(2).

Minuchin, S. 1974. *Families and Family Therapy.* Cambridge, MA: Harvard University Press.

Monahon, C. 1993. *Children and Trauma: A Parent's Guide to Helping Children Heal.* New York: Lexington Books.

Moos, R.H. 1990. *Coping Responses Inventory Manual.* Palo Alto, CA: Stanford University and Veterans Administration Medical Centers.

Moos, R.H., and A.G. Billings. 1982. "Conceptualizing and Measuring Coping Resources and Processes." In L. Goldberger and S. Breznitz (eds.), *Handbook of Stress: Theoretical and Clinical Aspects.* New York: The Free Press.

Muram, D., T.L. Rosenthal, and K.W. Beck. 1994. "Personality Profiles of Mothers of Sexual Abuse Victims and their Daughters." *Child Abuse and Neglect* 18.

Myer, M.H. 1985. "A New Look at Mothers of Incest Victims." *Journal of Social Work and Human Sexuality* 3.

Nadon, S.M. 1990. "Childhood Victimization: Antecedents to Prostitution." Paper presented at the Annual Convention of the Canadian Psychological Association, June, Ottawa, Ontario.

Naitove, C. 1982. "Arts Therapy With Sexually Abused Children." In S.M. Sgroi (ed.), *Handbook of Clinical Intervention in Child Sexual Abuse.* Lexington, MA: Lexington Books.

National Center for Missing and Exploited Children. 1997. *The Legal Validity and Policy Concerns Associated with Community Notification for Sex Offenders.* Arlington, VA: Author.

Nelson, C., and P. Jackson. 1989. "High-Risk Recognition: The Cognitive Behavioural Chain." In D.R. Laws (ed.), *Relapse Prevention with Sex Offenders.* New York: Guilford Press.

Newberger, C.M., I.M. Gremy, C.M. Waternaux and E.H. Newberger. 1993. "Mothers of Sexually Abused Children: Trauma and Repair in Longitudinal Perspective." *American Journal of Orthopsychiatry* 63.

Newton, E. 1996. "Power in Families and Power in Therapy: Child Sexual Abuse Survivors' Experiences." *Canadian Journal of Community Mental Health* 15.

O'Connor, K.J., and C.E. Schaefer. 1994. *Handbook of Play Therapy: Volume 2: Advances and Innovations.* New York: Wiley.

Ontario Native Women's Association. 1989. *Breaking Free: A Proposal for Change to Aboriginal Family Violence*. Thunder Bay: Ontario Native Women's Association.

Peake, A. 1987. "An Evaluation of Group Work for Sexually Abused Adolescent Girls and Boys." *Educational and Child Psychology* 4.

Pearlin, L.I., and C. Schooler. 1978. "The Structure of Coping." *Journal of Health and Social Behavior* 19.

Peterson, P. 1984. "Effects of Moderator Variables in Reducing Stress Outcome in Mothers of Children with Handicaps. *Journal of Psychosomatic Research* 28.

Peterson, R.F., S.M. Basta and T.A. Dykstra. 1993. "Mothers of Molested Children: Some Comparisons of Personality Characteristics." *Child Abuse and Neglect* 17.

Pierce, R., and L.H. Pierce. 1985. "The Sexually Abused Child: A Comparison of Male and Female Victims." *Child Abuse and Neglect* 9.

Porter, F.S., L.C. Blick and S.M. Sgroi. 1982. "Treatment of the Sexually Abused Child." In S.M. Sgroi (ed.), *Handbook of Clinical Intervention in Child Sexual Abuse*. Lexington, MA: Lexington Books.

Propst, L.R., A. Pardington, R. Ostrom and P. Watkins. 1986. "Predictions of Coping in Divorced Single Mothers." *Journal of Divorce* 9.

Raphling, D.L., B.L. Carpenter and A. Davis. 1967. "Incest: A Genealogical Study." *Archives of General Psychiatry* 16.

Reams, R., and W.N. Friedrich. 1994. "The Efficacy of Time-Limited Play Therapy With Maltreated Preschoolers." *Journal of Clinical Psychology* 50.

Reeker, J., D. Ensing and R. Elliott. 1997. "A Meta-Analytic Investigation of Group Treatment Outcomes for Sexually Abused Children." *Child Abuse and Neglect* 21.

Regehr, C. 1990. "Parental Responses to Extrafamilial Child Sexual Assault." *Child Abuse and Neglect* 14.

Reynolds, C.R., and B.O. Richmond. 1978. "What I Think and Feel: A Revised Measure of Children's Manifest Anxiety." *Journal of Abnormal Child Psychology* 6.

Rispens, J., A. Aleman and P.P. Goudena. 1997. "Prevention of Child Sexual Abuse Victimization: A Meta-Analysis of School Programs." *Child Abuse and Neglect* 21.

Robin, R.W., B. Chester, J.K. Rasmussen, J.N. Jaranson, and D. Goldman. 1997. "Prevalence, Characteristics, and Impact of Childhood Sexual Abuse in a Southwestern American Indian Tribe." *Child Abuse and Neglect* 21.

Rogers, C.M., and T. Terry. 1984. "Clinical Intervention with Boy Victims of Sexual Abuse." In I.R. Stuart and J.G. Greer (eds.), *Victims of Sexual Aggression: Treatment of Children, Women, and Men*. New York: Van Nostrand Reinhold.

Rogers, R.G. 1992. *Reaching for Solutions: The Report of the Special Advisor to the Minister of National Health and Welfare on Child Sexual Abuse in Canada*. Ottawa: Minister of Supply and Services Canada.

Romano, E. 1999. "Evaluation of a Multi-Component Individual Treatment Intervention for Adult Males with Histories of Sexual Abuse: A Multiple Baseline Approach." Unpublished doctoral dissertation, University of Manitoba, Winnipeg, Manitoba.

Romano, E., and R.V. De Luca. 1996. "Characteristics of Perpetrators with Histories of Sexual Abuse." *International Journal of Offender Therapy and Comparative Criminology* 40.

Romano, E., A.D. Grayston, R.V. De Luca and M.A. Gillis. 1996. "The Thematic Apperception Test as an Outcome Measure in the Treatment of Sexual Abuse: Preliminary Findings." *Journal of Child and Youth Care* 10(4).

Ruby, C., and D. Martin. 1997. *Criminal Sentencing Digest*. Markham: Butterworths Canada Ltd.

Rush, F. 1980. *The Best Kept Secret: Sexual Abuse of Children*. New York: McGraw Hill.

Russell, D.E.H. 1975. *The Politics of Rape*. New York: Stein and Day.

_____. 1983. "The Incidence and Prevalence of Intrafamilial and Extrafamilial Sexual Abuse of Female Children." *Child Abuse and Neglect* 7.

_____. 1984. *Sexual Exploitation: Rape, Child Sexual Abuse, and Workplace Harassment*. Beverly Hills, CA: Sage Publications.

_____. 1986. *The Secret Trauma: Incest in the Lives of Girls and Women*. New York: Basic Books.

Saunders, B.E., D.G. Kilpatrick, R.F. Hanson, H.S. Resnick and M.E. Walker. 1999. "Prevalence, Case Characteristics, and Long-Term Psychological Correlates of Child Rape among Women: A National Survey." *Child Maltreatment* 4.

Schaefer, C.E., and K.J. O'Connor. 1983. *Handbook of Play Therapy*. New York: Wiley.

Schram, D., and C. Milloy. 1995. *Community Notification: A Study of Offender Characteristics and Recidivism*. Seattle, WA: Washington State Institute for Public Policy.

Scott, R.L., and D.A. Stone. 1986. "MMPI Profile Constellations in Incest Families." *Journal of Consulting and Clinical Psychology* 54.

Selye, H. 1976. *The Stress of Life*. Revised edition. New York: McGraw-Hill.

Sgroi, S.M. 1982a. "Family Treatment of Child Sexual Abuse." *Journal of Social Work and Human Sexuality* 1.

_____. 1982b. *Handbook of Clinical Intervention in Child Sexual Abuse*. Lexington, Massachusetts: Lexington Books.

Shah, R.Z., P.W. Dail and T. Heinrichs. 1995. "Familial Influences upon the Occurrence of Childhood Sexual Abuse." *Journal of Child Sexual Abuse* 4(4).

Shapiro, J.P. 1991. "Interviewing Children about Psychological Issues Associated with Sexual Abuse." *Psychotherapy* 28.

Sirles, E.A., and P.J. Franke. 1989. "Factors Influencing Mothers' Reactions to Intrafamily Sexual Abuse." *Child Abuse and Neglect* 13.

Standing Committee on Justice and the Solicitor General. 1993. *Four-Year Review of the Child Sexual Abuse Provisions of the Criminal Code and the Canada Evidence Act (formerly Bill C-15)*. Ottawa: Supply and Services Canada.

Stevens, G., D. Fisher and L. Berg. 1992. *Review and Monitoring of Child Sexual Abuse Cases in Selected Sites in Saskatchewan*. Ottawa: Department of Justice.

Steward, M.S., L.C. Farquhar, D.C. Dicharry, D.R. Glick and P.W. Martin. 1986. "Group Therapy: A Treatment of Choice for Young Victims of Child Abuse." *International Journal of Group Psychotherapy* 36.

Strand, V.C. 1991. "Victim of Sexual Abuse: Case of Rosa, Age 6." In N.B. Webb (ed.), *Play Therapy With Children in Crisis: A Casebook for Practitioners.* New York: Guilford Press.

Sturkie, K. 1992. "Group Treatment of Child Sexual Abuse Victims: A Review." In W. O'Donohue and J.H. Geer (eds.), *The Sexual Abuse of Children: Clinical Issues: Volume 2.* Hillsdale, NJ: Lawrence Erlbaum.

Tamraz, D.N. 1996. "Nonoffending Mothers of Sexually Abused Children: Comparison of Opinions and Research." *Journal of Child Sexual Abuse* 5.

Timmons-Mitchell, J., D. Chandler-Holtz and W.E. Semple. 1996. "Post-Traumatic Stress Symptoms in Mothers following Children's Reports of Sexual Abuse: An Exploratory Study." *American Journal of Orthopsychiatry* 66.

Tingus, K.D., A.H. Heger, D.W. Foy and G.A. Leskin. 1996. "Factors Associated With Entry Into Therapy in Children Evaluated for Sexual Abuse." *Child Abuse and Neglect* 20.

Tong, L., K. Oates and M. McDowell. 1987. "Personality Development Following Sexual Abuse." *Child Abuse and Neglect* 11.

Tormes, Y.M. 1972. *Child Victims of Incest.* Denver: American Humane Association.

Trepper, T.S., and M.J. Barrett. 1989. *Systemic Treatment of Incest: A Therapeutic Handbook.* New York: Brunner/Mazel, Inc.

Truesdell, D.L., J.S. McNeil and J.P. Deschner. 1986. "Incidence of Wife Abuse in Incestuous Families." *Social Work* 31.

Trute, B., E. Adkins and G. MacDonald. 1994. *Coordinating Child Sexual Abuse Services in Rural Communities.* Toronto: University of Toronto Press.

Tutty, L.M. 1993. "Are Child Sexual Abuse Prevention Programs Effective?: A Review of the Research." *Sexological Review* 1(2).

Ursel, J. 1992a. *Private Lives, Public Policy: 100 Years of State Intervention in the Family.* Toronto: Women's Press.

_____. 1992b. *Winnipeg Family Violence Court: Final Report: Year One.* Winnipeg: Criminology Research Centre, Department of Sociology, University of Manitoba.

Vogeltanz, N.D., S.C. Wilsnack, T.R. Harris, R.W. Wilsnack, S.A. Wonderlich and A.F. Kristjanson. 1999. "Prevalence and Risk Factors for Childhood Sexual Abuse in Women: National Survey Findings." *Child Abuse and Neglect* 23.

Wagner, W.G. 1991. "Depression in Mothers of Sexually Abused vs. Mothers of Nonabused Children." *Child Abuse and Neglect* 15.

Walker, L.E.A., and M.A. Bolkovatz. 1988. "Play Therapy with Children Who Have Experienced Sexual Assault." In L.E.A. Walker (ed.), *Handbook on Sexual Abuse of Children: Assessment and Treatment Issues.* New York: Springer.

Ward, E. 1984. *Father–Daughter Rape.* London: The Women's Press.

Waterman, J., and R. Lusk. 1993. "Psychological Testing in Evaluation of Child Sexual Abuse." *Child Abuse and Neglect* 17.

Wattenberg, E. 1985. "In a Different Light: A Feminist Perspective on the Role of Mothers in Father–Daughter Incest." *Child Welfare* 64.

Webb, N.B. 1991. "Play Therapy Crisis Intervention with Children." In N.B. Webb (ed.), *Play Therapy With Children in Crisis: A Casebook for Practitioners.* New York: Guilford.

Weiner, I.B. 1962. "Father–Daughter Incest: A Clinical Report." *Psychiatric Quarterly* 36.

Wells, M. 1990. *Canada's Law on Child Sexual Abuse*. Ottawa: Department of Justice.

White, S., B.M. Halpin, G.A. Strom and G. Santilli. 1988. "Behavioral Comparisons of Young Sexually Abused, Neglected, and Nonreferred Children." *Journal of Clinical Child Psychology* 17.

Williams, L.M. 1994. "Recall of Childhood Trauma: A Prospective Study of Women's Memories of Child Sexual Abuse." *Journal of Consulting and Clinical Psychology* 62.

Wolf, M.M. 1978. "Social Validity: The Case for Subjective Measurement or How Applied Behavior Analysis is Finding its Heart." *Journal of Applied Behavior Analysis* 11.

Wolfe, V.V., and J. Birt. 1995. "The Psychological Sequelae of Child Sexual Abuse." In T.H. Ollendick and R.J. Prinz (eds.), *Advances in Clinical Psychology: Volume 17*. New York: Plenum.

Wolfe, V.V., and C. Gentile. 1992. "Psychological Assessment of Sexually Abused Children." In W. O'Donohue and J.H. Geer (eds.), *The Sexual Abuse of Children: Clinical Issues: Volume 2*. Hillsdale, NJ: Erlbaum.

Wurtele, S.K. 1998. "School-Based Child Sexual Abuse Prevention Programs: Questions, Answers, and More Questions." In J.R. Lutzker (ed.), *Handbook of Child Abuse Research and Treatment*. New York: Plenum.

Wyatt, G.E. 1985. "The Sexual Abuse of Afro-American and White-American Women in Childhood." *Child Abuse and Neglect* 9.

Wyckoff, P., and M.T. Erickson. 1987. "Mediating Factors of Stress on Mothers of Seriously Ill, Hospitalized Children." *Children's Health Care* 16.

Young, A.H. 1992. "Child Sexual Abuse and the Law of Evidence: Some Current Canadian Issues." *Canadian Journal of Family Law* 2.

Young, S. 1997. "The Use of Normalization as a Strategy in the Sexual Exploitation of Children by Adult Offenders." *The Canadian Journal of Human Sexuality* 6.

Zuelzer, M.B., and R.E. Reposa. 1983. "Mothers in Incestuous Families." *International Journal of Family Therapy* 5.

Hurting and Healing: A Series on Intimate Violence

The Hurting and Healing series on intimate violence is a project of RESOLVE a tri-provincial research network on family violence. RESOLVE (Research and Education for Solutions to Violence and Abuse) is committed to conducting and encouraging pragmatic program and policy based research in partnership with community agencies. We have offices in Winnipeg, Saskatoon and Calgary and partnerships with seven prairie universities and a broad range of community based agencies in each province. Our Hurting and Healing book series reflects the philosophy of our organization with partner editors and contributors from the university and the community.

The increasing disclosure of violence in families and intimate relations poses many questions for practitioners and policy-makers. What is the most effective way to intervene and stop the intergenerational cycle of violence? Does criminalization help or make matters worse? Can family violence offenders be rehabilitated? Most importantly; How can we prevent the violence from happening in the first place? Over the years our research projects have grappled with these issues. In the Hurting and Healing series we will be sharing the results of some of our studies with you. We hope that our books will be useful to practitioners and researchers alike.

We are very proud of this second volume and hope you will look for the first and third book in our series:

Summer 2000 Volume 1
No Place for Violence: Canadian Aboriginal Alternatives
Jocelyn Proulx and Sharon Perrault (Manitoba)
136pp ISBN:1-55266-034-6 $15.95

Spring 2002 Volume 3
Women Abused by Intimate Partners: Challenges and Solutions
edited by Leslie Tutty (Social Work, University of Calgary) and
Carolyn Goard (Sheriff King Family Support Centre, Calgary)